Business & Environmental Ethics

Ethics Study Guide

Peter Baron

First published 2014

by PushMe Press

Mid Somerset House, Southover, Wells, Somerset BA5 1UH

www.pushmepress.com

© 2014 Inducit Learning Ltd

British Library Cataloguing in Publication Data
A catalogue record for this book is available from the British Library

ISBN: 978-1-909618-26-8 (pbk)
ISBN: 978-1-78484-005-1 (hbk)
ISBN: 978-1-909618-27-5 (ebk)
ISBN: 978-1-78484-006-8 (pdf)

Typeset in Frutiger by booksellerate.com
Printed by Lightning Source

A rich & engaging community assisted by the best teachers in Ethics

ethics.pushmepress.com

Students and teachers explore Ethics through handouts, film clips, presentations, case studies, extracts, games and academic articles.

Pitched just right, and so much more than a text book, here is a place to engage with critical reflection whatever your level. Marked student essays are also posted.

Contents

Four Issues in Environmental Ethics

Environmental Ethics forgoes the luxury of pursuing happiness, recognising the stark fact that physical survival takes precedence over all else in the order of ethical concerns, regardless of whatever martyrdom we subsequently contemplate. (Shirk, 1998: 80)

Is the human race committing collective suicide with behaviour that produces irreversible effects on the natural world? Are we dying the death of a pursuit of short-term happiness and local interests? Can ethical theories cope with the requirement to find and educate people into new and costly obligations to the environment?

Physical survival is surely a basic moral precept that trumps all others. Global temperatures are forecast to rise between 1° and 5°C by 2100. The ice sheet (so the argument goes) melts at the poles and ocean levels rise. As ocean levels rise countries at low sea levels flood. At the same time, climate becomes more unstable - some areas turn to desert, other areas flood. The acidity of the sea rises as water absorbs the increased CO_2. Ocean species (such as coral) start to die. Moreover the climate changes have political impacts as population migrates to cooler parts of the world. These are just some of the potential consequences of climate change indicated by global warming activists.

This book is not about ecology or geography or meteorology. It's about ethics: the study of right actions and the idea of what is good or desirable and how humans ought to behave. The study of ethics, however, includes facts - what we call **NATURALISM** in ethics links the idea of goodness to certain natural features of the world. The question is begged, what is there about the environment that has moral worth? Is there anything intrinsically good about nature? Are some human activities which affect the environment - cutting down the rainforest, releasing CO2 through coal fired power stations, or even the decision to have 13 children and so increase the world population - seen to be wrong? Or is something like family size morally neutral? Is it up to me what car I drive, or is it wrong to drive a car which does only 18 mpg? Does it matter if the world population is forecast to peak at around 11 billion?

What makes the study of the environment complex is that it includes both economic and political factors. The US Government has failed to sign up to carbon reduction treaties like Kyoto. US petrol prices are 50% lower than in Europe. China is building one new coal fired power station a week. One US Senator, James Inhofe, described global warming predictions as 'the biggest hoax ever perpetrated on the US people'. David Attenborough, the British naturalist, has commented recently:

> I think it's very sad that people won't accept evidence for what it says—it's extraordinary that one of the wealthiest, materially advanced societies in the world can support irrational myths in that way. That they should do it privately is up to them but since what they do effects that whole world it's pretty serious that they should not accept that humanity has been responsible for these changes that are absolutely evident to everyone else. (Feb 2014)

ISSUE 1 - ANTHROPOCENTRIC V HOLISTIC THEORIES

In the debate on environmental issues we find three circles of value (Fig 1).

ANTHROPOCENTRIC - (human-centred) in the centre, a narrow field of value places moral worth only on human life and all other species and the biotic community generally have value only as a means to human welfare, what we call **INSTRUMENTAL VALUE**. Traditional ethical theories (Kant, Natural Law, Utilitarian) are seen as anthropocentric as they stress human rationality and human ends as the source of moral value.

BIOCENTRIC - (life-centred) sees a wider circle of value existing in the biosphere, which includes all individual living entities, from animal species to plants and trees.

ECO-HOLISTIC - (one ecosystem) the biosphere has value because of its interdependence and integrity. It should be viewed as a single entity, like a human body, rather than separate life-forms.

Environmentalists challenge traditional ethical theories which seem to give a morally superior place to humans and in some cases, discount the environment altogether. If we decide to argue for the **INTRINSIC** value of the natural world, how do we derive this value? It has to come from somewhere and secondly, we have to motivate human beings to accept and follow its principles. Is this asking too much? Can the Land Ethic of Leopold, or the eco-holistic ethic of James Lovelock's Gaia theory give us a convincing case for arguing that the environment is good in itself?

Figure 1: Circles of Value

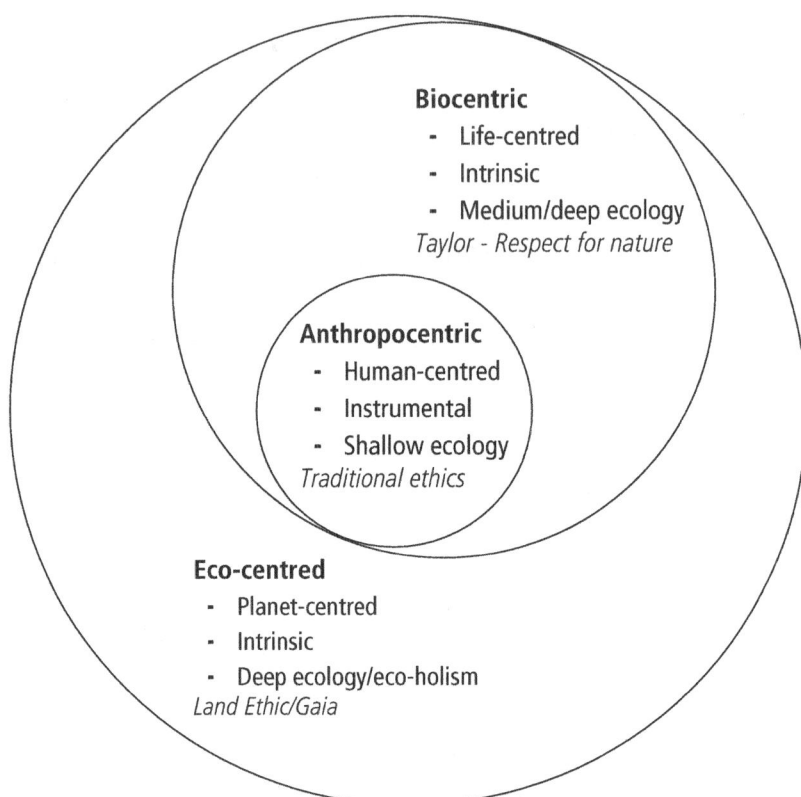

Other theorists like John Passmore have argued for a form of **ENLIGHTENED ANTHROPOCENTRISM**. Traditional theories such as Utilitarianism, Kantian ethics or Natural Law which place humanity at the pinnacle of a moral system, can perhaps be successfully adapted to include the principle of 'no harm to others'. The 'no harm' here can be widened to include 'no long-term harm to the welfare of other species'. William Grey puts this like this:

We need to reject not anthropocentrism, but a particularly short term and narrow conception of human interests and concerns. What's wrong with shallow anthropocentric views is not their concern about the well-being of humans, but that they do not really consider enough in what that well-being consists. We need to develop an enriched, fortified anthropocentric notion of human interest to replace the dominant short-term, sectional and self-regarding conception. Grey, "Anthropocentrism and Deep Ecology", Australasian Journal of Philosophy 71: no 4, December 1993.

In later sections I consider how modern Kantians such as Christine Korsgaard develop the concept of **INDIRECT DUTIES** to the environment. I consider how Utilitarian ethics in the hands of Peter Singer embraces the idea of animal rights and ecological interests, and Natural Law (evidenced by papal encyclicals such as Caritas in Veritate (2009) or Veritatis Splendor (1995)) develops the **PRIMARY PRECEPT** of preservation of life to include ideas of stewardship of the natural world.

In contrast, environmental eco-holistics such as John Baird Callicott (in the tradition of Leopold's Land Ethic) have called upon philosophers to try to come up with a super-theory that embraces everything - from human species to the biotic world.

ISSUE 2 - INTRINSIC V INSTRUMENTAL GOODNESS

In 1949 Aldo Leopold produced a detailed statement of value for the biotic community - the community of all living things. He came up with a new moral principle: 'A thing is right when it tends to preserve the integrity, stability and beauty of the biotic community. It is wrong when it tends otherwise'. Leopold's statement neatly brought together a sense of aesthetic value (beauty) and moral value (integrity and stability) based on the idea that things that seem disparate were in fact interdependent.

If a tree also has some value in itself independently of the way it relates to some other ends such as human health, or the pleasure from seeing something beautiful, then the tree is said to have intrinsic value. This also generates a direct moral duty to protect it or at least refrain from doing it harm. What is the source of this intrinsic value? Biocentrists like Paul Taylor (1986) argue it lies in the individual living thing, and eco-holists like Lovelock (1949) in the entire ecosystem. Leopold can therefore be described as an **ECO-HOLIST**, whereas Taylor is a **BIOCENTRIST**. But it is to Leopold that we owe a debt for pointing out that value may exist in systems of living things, and not just individual species.

In 1976 the philosopher Richard Routley described the following thought experiment. Suppose you're the last person alive after a global catastrophe, and you have the power to destroy all that's left of nature. There is no-one left to suffer the disutility of the loss. Routley argues that we feel intuitively that it would still be wrong to destroy the natural world. Doesn't this suggest that nature has intrinsic value, regardless of the instrumental value to humans? Mustn't we respect nature because it is morally right to do so, not because of some benefit it gives us?

ISSUE 3 - POPULATION GROWTH AND OUR PLACE IN NATURE

Human beings have grown numerically, primarily due to the industrial revolution and scientific progress on health. The world population is forecast to peak at around 11 billion, not because of increased birth rates, but because survival and life expectancy has shot up. In the UK for example, ten years has been added to life expectancy in thirty years.

Such a rapid rise in population puts enormous strain on the biosphere. Forests are cut down for agriculture; oceans are overfished; farming techniques relying on man-made fertilisers pollute rivers and poison lakes. Species suffer from the changing ecosystem. Moreover, conflicts of interest arise at many levels.

Can we give rights to other species and living organisms to protect them in the face of population growth? In his book Respect For Nature, Paul

Taylor defends a **BIOCENTRIC EGALITARIANISM** in which all living organisms have rights. But rights, if they exist, often conflict. The rights of the cattle in Devon conflict with the rights of badgers who are blamed for spreading tuberculosis. The rights of trees conflict with the needs of human begins for building materials. Paul Taylor's priority principles discussed below aim to provide a way of judging between such conflicts.

Natural evolution has seen many species die out, and it might very well be the case that some species cannot coexist with other species. Moreover, it seems that if the larger animals are to survive in the future, it will be because humans protect their habitat. This places us in the role of stewards of nature, not just biological creatures acting in ways determined by evolution. But if humans are placed in charge of species' survival, it seems we are assigning ourselves a very special role in nature – a dominant role at odds with biocentic egalitarianism.

ISSUE 4 - MORAL STATUS OF FUTURE GENERATIONS

We have seen that some philosophers argue for a super-theory of everything - a moral theory that embraces all living things. Arguably, Gaia theory, for example, which is primarily a scientific view based on a holistic assumption, could be adapted into one such all-embracing moral theory. And of Aldo Leopold, the Stanford Encyclopaedia comments:

> *Leopold himself provided no systematic ethical theory or framework to support these ethical ideas concerning the environment. His views therefore presented a challenge and opportunity for moral theorists: could some ethical theory be devised to justify the injunction to preserve the integrity, stability and beauty of the biosphere?*

This super-theory (should we find an adequate one) urgently needs to address the problem of future generations, yet unborn. Utilitarianism fails here, as it can only account for the happiness or pleasure of living beings (as we shall see, it can, however, include animals in its moral compass). Kantian ethics relies on universalising behaviour to produce **CATEGORICALS** - rules that must be obeyed unconditionally, without exception. To universalise for the future entails certainty about what the planet will look like in 100 years time. But there is no way of knowing for certain what the complex effects of global warming will be.

For example, if the warm gulf stream currents change direction as the ice flow melts and cooler water flows south, Britain could end up with a climate, not like the South of France (as some predicted) but more like Norway. Natural Law theory faces similar problems: preservation of life is a key precept in Natural Law, but whose life? Should we care more about the poverty of those on the edge of the Amazon rainforest, (who would like to cut it down) or some future generation who need its supply of oxygen?

Aldo Leopold's Land Ethic

ECO-HOLISM implies treating nature as an interdependent whole, where preservation of the life of the whole overrides the interest of any particular species or individual. As the Encyclopaedia of Environmental Ethics puts it : 'holism asserts that the whole is greater than the sum of its parts'. It is normally contrasted with **REDUCTIONISM** which implies that 'the experienced world is only understandable through its component parts'.

A central figure in the eco-holism movement in the twentieth century was Aldo Leopold (1887-1949), a wilderness ranger and then Professor at Wisconsin University, who bought a shack in the Sand County and in 1949 wrote a series of meditations on the changing seasons called A Sand County Almanac.

Aldo Leopold recounts how, whilst out hunting as a forest warden in 1940, he killed a she-wolf with cubs. He sees this as a moment of conversion to what became later known as his Land Ethic.

> *We reached the old wolf in time to see the fierce green fire dying in her eyes. I realised then, and have known ever since that there was something new to me in her eyes - something known only to her and to the mountain. (1949:130)*

Leopold discovers a new respect for the wolf, and her relation to the land, and of human beings' relation to the wolf. The dying wolf is an enemy to the individual deer it kills to eat, but a friend of the deer species and so also, by extension, friend to the forest and the mountain. For without the wolf the deer would not be the agile, super-sensory organism we have today, and without the wolf the forest would be overgrazed and its ability to replenish itself would be compromised by the overpopulation of deer that eat the saplings. This **INTERDEPENDENCY** therefore becomes the foundation of his eco-holism: the idea of a 'biotic community' is greater than the sum of the parts (species) that make up that community.

The concept of "wilderness" also took on a new meaning in Aldo Leopold's conversion to a **LAND ETHIC**; rather than a hunting or recreational ground, it becomes an arena for a healthy **BIOTIC COMMUNITY**. So in 1935, Leopold helped found the Wilderness Society, dedicated to expanding and protecting America's wilderness areas. He quotes Georges Thoreau with approval - 'in wilderness lies the salvation of the world' - because wilderness gives us a sense of our place in nature, and is the foundation of a new humility.

Leopold's genius was to combine a poetic mysticism with the hard scientific facts of ecology and a new ethic of human behaviour. This ethic is based on a number of premises.

FOUR PREMISES OF THE LAND ETHIC

1. **A METAPHYSICAL PREMISE** of the idea of land as community. Leopold writes 'land as a community is the basic concept of ecology'. In recognising this concept of land as community 'we begin to treat it with love and respect' (1949:viii). Human beings form part of this community, but without any privileged position. The 'community' is a metaphysical idea, greater than the sum of its biological parts.

2. **A SCIENTIFIC PREMISE** of the idea of land health. Leopold doesn't attempt to prove the desirability of land health - he argues that health is desirable in itself. Conservation therefore can be defined as retaining or restoring the ability of the land to heal itself: 'health is the capacity of the land for self-renewal', he writes. Putting hard facts on the concept of land health gives ecology a scientific basis.

3. **AN ANTHROPOLOGICAL PREMISE** of human beings as community members who exist as parts of a greater whole. The 'whole' defines the idea of the good (see Figure 1 above). Entailed by this is a new sense of what it is to be human.

4. **An ethical premise** of love and respect for the land born of a sense of wonder. Leopold calls this an ethical relation to the land.

It is inconceivable to me that an ethical relation to land can exist without love, respect, and admiration for land, and a high regard for its value. By value, I of course mean something far broader than mere economic value; I mean value in the philosophical sense. (1949:211)

THE PYRAMID OF LIFE

Aldo Leopold replaces the idea of a 'balance of nature' with the idea of a **PYRAMID OF LIFE** which has evolved with the evolution of humankind. The pyramid started flat and relatively simple and then evolved over millennia into something of increasing height and complexity with the evolution of different species.

At the top of the pyramid is human life - conscious and making choices - which has learnt to treat the land as something to be exploited. Then we have different species of animals and mammals, fish and birds, but at the base of the pyramid is the land itself. Hence a land ethic is an attitude of respect for the basis of all life. The land sustains the biotic community.

How does the land do this? The land, taking its energy from the sun and from water, is itself the energy source for all life. On the land a hierarchy of species is built, with each dependent on the other. The health of the soil itself determines the health of the species above it. The food chains that emanate from the land depend on this 'conduit of energy', as he calls it.

Leopold points out that human changes operate quickly whereas the pyramid of life and energy has emerged slowly by millennia of evolution. 'Man's invention of tools has enabled him to make changes of unprecedented violence, rapidity, and scope', and we reap 'the penalties for our violence' (1949:240). The food chain becomes shorter and also energy is transferred more quickly by use of power and artificial fertilisers. Species go rapidly into decline or are made extinct by human activity.

The concept of a 'catastrophic cascade' is explained in the chapter, "Thinking Like a Mountain". Here Leopold realises that killing a predator wolf carries serious implications for the rest of the ecosystem. The death of the wolf entails the death of the forest as the deer, without their natural predator, destroy trees. So we need to value **HARMONY** where "conservation is a state of harmony between men and land". This involves developing a new affinity for the land and a new love and respect for it. In a particularly poetic passage of the Sand County Almanac he writes:

> *This sounds simple: do we not already sing our love for and obligation to the land of the free and the home of the brave? Yes, but just what and whom do we love? Certainly not the soil, which we are sending helter-skelter down river. Certainly not the waters, which we assume have no function except to turn turbines, float barges, and carry off sewage. Certainly not the plants, of which we exterminate whole communities without batting an eye. Certainly not the animals, of which we have already extirpated many of the largest and most beautiful species. A land ethic of course cannot prevent the alteration, management, and use of these 'resources,' but it does affirm their right to continued existence, and, at least in spots, their continued existence in a natural state. In short, a land ethic changes the role of Homo sapiens from conqueror of the land-community to plain member and citizen of it. It implies respect for his fellow-members, and also respect for the community as such. (1949:243)*

A NEW ETHIC AND A NEW SET OF DUTIES

One of the best-known quotes from the Sand County Almanac clarifies three sources of value in Leopold's land ethic, which in turn create three duties:

> *A thing is right when it tends to preserve the integrity, stability, and beauty of the biotic community. It is wrong when it tends otherwise. (1949:262)*

What is meant by each of the terms 'stability', 'integrity' and 'beauty" which determine the rightness of our actions? And what duties do they imply?

Duty 1 - To protect the stability of the ecosystem.

The idea of stability has invited criticism because it suggest that the environment is unchanging or static. However, it suggests the idea of health mentioned as one of the premises in his argument. Land health is defined as the ability of the land to sustain and regenerate itself: 'land is stable when its food chains can circulate the same food an indefinite number of times' (1999:205). So one example of the 'violence' humans can do to the land is excessive deforestation. The earth erodes and washes away and so the land becomes useless for cultivation and also unable to regenerate itself. The violence human beings do to the land is thus a form of suicide. To kill the land is to kill ourselves.

Duty 2 - To preserve the integrity of the biosphere.

What does the word 'integrity' mean? Does it mean we are to leave the land untouched, as we found it? Integrity implies 'wholeness' and 'integration'. The land ethic is the ethic of the whole ecosystem, not the human part we traditionally concentrate on in our anthropocentric human ethics. So integrity implies retaining all the species necessary to protect the stability of the food chain. 'A land ethic', he asserts, 'implies respect for fellow-members and for the community as such' (1949:204).

Duty 3 - To stir up the kind of feelings of 'affirmation, love and well-being' that stem from a sense of wonder at nature and its beauty.

Leopold's third element invokes the idea of beauty. But what is beauty? George Santayanna defines beauty as 'pleasure objectified'. It may have an evolutionary basis in the sense of wonder human beings possess in the mystery of our own environment and the ability we have to turn nature into a god to be worshipped. This will involve a fundamental change, argues Leopold, in our 'affirmations, loyalties, and convictions' (1949:210) - we will need to look at nature in a new way and respond appropriately.

This includes the wilderness which may have little or no economic value.

A NEW IDEA OF WHAT IT IS TO BE HUMAN

Behind his land ethic with its new set of duties Leopold is presenting a new idea of what it means to be human. He blames the Abrahamic religions for their obsession with the idea of land as a resource to be used instrumentally to generate wealth. Central to this is the idea of property and ownership:

> *The first ethics dealt with the relation between individuals; the Mosaic Decalogue is an example. Later accretions dealt with the relation between the individual and society. The Golden Rule tries to integrate the individual to society; democracy to integrate social organisation to the individual. There is as yet no ethic dealing with man's relation to land and to the animals and plants which grow upon it. Land, like Odysseus' slave-girls, is still property. The land-relation is still strictly economic, entailing privileges but not obligations. (1949:248)*

He replaces this, as we have seen, with the idea of land as community to be respected and valued in itself. Human begins are now seen as members of the biotic community and 'fellow-citizens', rather than rulers of nature and 'superior'. Community and co-operation evolve together and 'the land ethic simply enlarges the boundaries of the community to include soils, waters, plants, and animals, or collectively: the land'.

The foundation value is therefore respect - **RESPECT FOR NATURE**. Contrary to some forms of the Christian tradition, the role of human beings is not to exploit and subjugate nature, but respect it. This respect extends to private landowners who need to see themselves as custodians and stewards of the land. Leopold criticises such landowners and argues for a role for Governments in regulating and tempering their conduct:

'when the private landowner is asked to perform some unprofitable act for the good of the community, he today assents only with outstretched palm'. We need to shift from conquerors to 'plain members' of the biotic community who have a conscience for 'obligations which have no meaning without conscience', and 'the problem we face is the extension of the social conscience from people to land.'

> In human history, we have learned (I hope) that the conqueror role is eventually self-defeating. Why? Because it is implicit in such a role that the conqueror knows, like one infallible, just what makes the community clock tick; and just what and who is valuable, and what and who is worthless, in community life. It always turns out that he knows neither, and this is why his conquests eventually defeat themselves. (1949:246)

ORIGINS IN DARWINISM

Aldo Leopold argues for an ethical viewpoint that evolves with the evolution of humankind and is still evolving to meet new challenges.

> *This extension of ethics, so far studied only by philosophers, is actually a process in ecological evolution. Its sequences may be described in ecological as well as in philosophical terms. An ethic, ecologically, is a limitation on freedom of action in the struggle for existence. An ethic, philosophically, is a differentiation of social from anti-social conduct. These are two definitions of one thing. The thing has its origin in the tendency of interdependent individuals or groups to evolve modes of co-operation. (1949:202)*

Here Leopold places himself firmly in the Darwinist tradition of evolutionary ethics championed in our time by Richard Dawkins. Darwin argued that 'no tribe could hold together if murder, robbery, treachery were common' (Descent of Man) and the basis for this is **SYMPATHY** and the understanding of mutual dependency. Ethics for Darwin is a means of social co-operation needed to face the struggle for survival more successfully. Sympathies developed and were gradually extended, from family to extended family to tribe, to groups of tribes, and to the nation as a whole. Darwin believed that the process could extend (with sympathy and imagination) to the whole world. He wrote: "there is only an artificial barrier to stop his sympathies being extended to the men of all nations and races".

Leopold's Land Ethic has exactly the same evolutionary emphasis grounded in social co-operation: 'the tendency of interdependent individuals or groups to evolve means of co-operation' (1949:202).

Darwin saw that it required the development of intelligence and imagination to understand the consequences of antisocial behaviour. Leopold argues for a new consciousness and a changed conscience based on the understanding of the interdependence of human and non-human life, whereby every individual takes responsibility for human choice and doesn't just leave it to the government to regulate and legislate for conservation. In the tradition of David Hume sympathy is the key attitude - sympathy that goes well beyond a feeling for our fellow human beings to the very land itself.

TWO ISSUES ARISING

Aldo Leopold sees two major issues arising from his ethic - one to do with the adjustment of the land to human activity and the other to do with the amount of 'violence' we mete out upon the land.

Can the land adjust itself to the new order? Can the desired alterations be accomplished with less violence? (1949:203)

1. The less violent (destructive, mechanised) the man-made changes, the greater the probability of successful readjustment in the pyramid. Violence, in turn, varies with human population density; a dense population requires a more violent conversion. So population and overpopulation issues are ethically important.

2. It depends on the area where you live whether the changes can be affected without violence. Deforestation for example affects different areas of the world in different ways - depending on the local climate an the ability of other plant life to limit erosion.

This almost world-wide display of disorganization in the land seems to be similar to disease in an animal, except that it never culminates in complete disorganization or death. The land recovers, but at some reduced level of complexity, and with a reduced carrying capacity for people, plants, and animals: many biotas currently regarded as 'lands of opportunity' are in fact already subsisting on exploitative agriculture, i.e. they have already exceeded their sustained carrying capacity. (1949:210)

Conservation means restoring the ability of the land to heal itself.

CONCLUSION

Leopold's own words elegantly capture his conclusions in his own poetic language:

> *A system of conservation based solely on economic self-interest is hopelessly lopsided. It tends to ignore, and thus eventually to eliminate, many elements in the land community that lack commercial value, but that are (as far as we know) essential to its healthy functioning. It assumes, falsely, I think, that the economic -parts of the biotic clock will function without the uneconomic parts. It tends to relegate to government many functions eventually too large, too complex, or too widely dispersed to be performed by government. An ethical obligation on the part of the private owner is the only visible remedy for these situations.*

> *In all of these cleavages, we see repeated the same basic paradoxes: man the conqueror versus man the biotic citizen; science the sharpener of his sword versus science the searchlight on his universe; land the slave and servant versus land the collective organism. Robinson's injunction to Tristram may well be applied, at this juncture, to Homo Sapiens as a species in geological time.*

> *Whether you will or not You are a King, Tristram, for you are one of the time-tested few that leave the world, when they are gone, not the same place it was. Mark what you leave. (1949: 212)*

EVALUATION

Intrinsic or instrumental?

Scholars argue about whether Leopold is arguing for intrinsic value of the biotic community. J. Baird Callicott thinks he is, Paul Taylor thinks he isn't. Callicott argues that Leopold is creating duties to care for the land - it is a deontological ethic grounded in a theory of intrinsic value. Norton, in contrast, argues that Leopold links the land ethic to long-term human flourishing and so it retains an essentially instrumental focus. As Eric Freyfogle (Encyclopaedia page 23) observes, 'the community is simply the soundest practical focus for promoting human flourishing' .

Eco-fascism?

Does this entail a sort of ecological fascism whereby populations are deliberately reduced or relocated? If the biotic community is superior to the human community, what happens when the interests of each clash? How do we attach moral value to something as intangible as the land community? A human population of 7 billion forecast to rise to 11 billion within 200 years is clearly a threat to the integrity, stability and beauty of the biotic community. William Aiken argues that according to the land ethic 'massive human die backs would be good. It is our species duty, relative to the whole, to eliminate 90% of our numbers'. (1984:269)

What is this 'community'?

Community is ill-defined in Leopold's writings. Community implies rights and obligations. But does it make sense to see the land having an obligation to us? And what exactly is our moral obligation to preserve the land when we cannot feed our children? Is it realistic to have this egalitarian emphasis when common sense seems to suggest that human beings will always consider their own interest above that of nature - until it can be proved that it is in our interest to preserve nature? But then we are forced back to arguing for an instrumental environmental ethic on utilitarian grounds.

Gaia Theory as Eco-holism

In his 2009 book, The Vanishing Face of Gaia, James Lovelock defined Gaia as:

> *A view of the earth as a self-regulating system made up from the totality of all organisms, the surface rocks, the oceans and the atmosphere tightly coupled as an evolving system, and having a goal - the regulation of surface conditions so as always to be favourable to life. (2009:166)*

According to a recent book by a British scientist Toby Tyrell (2013:7), we can reduce this hypothesis to three statements which are testable scientifically:

1. **LIFE-ENHANCING** - the environment is very well suited to the organisms that inhabit it. Tolerances for temperature (within 5 degrees), Oxygen (21% of atmosphere) and salinity (3.4% concentration) are exactly right for biotic life.

2. **UNIQUE** - the Earth's atmosphere is a biological construct whose composition is far from expectations of chemical equilibrium. For example, given the concentration of methane on Earth, which absorbs oxygen, the level of oxygen is higher than expected.

3. **STABLE** - The Earth has been a stable environment over time, despite various external 'shocks".

For example the evolution of the planet has included various catastrophes and extinctions: these include meteor strikes, volcanic eruptions (the eruptions of 1788 are said to have been instrumental as a cause of the food shortages that sparked the French Revolution), and changes in solar energy.

A global warming occurred 14,000 years ago when the planet warmed by 5°C and sea levels rose 100 metres. But the earth's interdependent biotic system - a complex mixture of gasses, minerals and organisms - acts as one giant **SUPERORGANISM** which generally reacts to restore a new equilibrium. That is the scientific claim of James Lovelock, originator of the Gaia hypothesis, who asks us to view the entire biota, animal and plant life, and ecosystem - including rocks and minerals - as one giant interdependent body.

Tyrell also points out, following earlier work by James Kirchner, that the Gaia hypothesis is ambiguous as an idea and that Lovelock has modified his version in crucial ways. Reading the strongest forms of Gaian theory first, we find for example, the following emphases:

1. **OPTIMISING GAIA**, which argues that the biosphere is optimised in favour of the biota (2003:6).

2. **TELEOLOGICAL GAIA**, which implies that the biosphere has a purpose - to optimise conditions for life.

3. **HOMEOSTATIC GAIA**, which emphasises the stabilising effect of the biota. In 1974 Lovelock wrote, citing fossil records as evidence, of 'homeostasis on a planetary scale maintained by life on the surface' (1974:93)

4. **CO-EVOLUTIONARY GAIA**, which sees the biota influencing the non-biotic environment by a Darwinian mechanism of

evolution. By 1983 Lovelock was writing of 'two parts of a coupled system', (1983:284).

Lovelock has abandoned the emphases of the stronger versions (1&2) - of optimising intention and conscious purpose, in favour of the third more descriptive (and hence scientific-sounding) version which emphasises **HOMEOSTASIS**. So Lovelock's later definition (2009) quoted above replaces 'optimal' with 'favourable' and although he talks about a 'goal', the goal does not have conscious intent. Lovelock concludes as early as 1987 in preface to a new edition of his 1979 book:

> *Gaia does not optimise the environment for life. I should have said that it keeps the environment constant and close to a state comfortable for life. (1987)*

In fact Gaia (unlike Leopold's Land Ethic) presents a new model of evolution which may explain why Darwinists like Richard Dawkins dislike it. In the Darwinian scheme of thought, plants and animals react to changes brought about by catastrophic events such as volcanic eruption that wiped out Neanderthal man 25,000 years ago as the earth cooled. But according to the Gaia hypothesis, the effects of the earth evolve together in certain interdependent feedback loops. The result is that Lovelock argues, in Toby Tyrrell's words, that 'life has had a hand on the tiller of environmental control' (2013:4):

> *The physical and chemical condition of the surface of the Earth, of the atmosphere, and of the oceans has been and is actively made fit and comfortable by the presence of life itself. This is in contrast to the conventional wisdom which held that life adapted to the planetary conditions as it and they evolved their separate ways. (1987:152)*

The analogy is of the human body. Just as all the cells of the human body interact and coordinate to preserve the life of the body as a whole, so the different elements of **BIOTA** and ecosystems of the Earth interact and co-ordinate to regulate certain variables in such a way as to sustain life. Gaia, at least in early formulations of the Gaia hypothesis, is teleological - there is a purpose or as Lovelock's 2009 definition puts it, a goal. That goal is to maintain the conditions that support biotic life.

And what are these conditions? They are conditions of **HOMEOSTASIS**, meaning a steady state. Despite the increase of the sun's temperature by 25°C since the foundation of Gaia, the global temperature has only risen by 5°C. If the self-regulating mechanisms had not kicked in, the effect would have been an initial rise in temperature, followed by fall in temperature to minus 19°C. The feedback processes are unconscious but nonetheless inbuilt:

> *The Gaia hypothesis says that the temperature, oxidation state, acidity, and certain aspects of the rocks and waters are kept constant, and that this homeostasis is maintained by active feedback processes operated automatically and unconsciously by the biota.(1979: xx)*

At other times the increase in the sun's temperature has produced Greenhouse gasses, quite naturally, which have warmed the earth up. So Gaia has both cooling and warming powers, like a thermostat linked to a boiler and an air-conditioning unit at the same time. The conclusion in Lovelock's own words is that:

> *The notion of the biosphere as active adaptive control system able to maintain the earth in homeostasis we are calling the Gaia hypothesis. (1974:3)*

More poetically he addresses his critics:

> I recognise that to view the Earth as if it were alive is just a convenient, but different, way of organising the facts of the Earth. I am of course prejudiced in favour of Gaia and have filled my life for the past twenty-five years with the thought that Earth may be alive: not as the ancients saw her—a sentient Goddess with a purpose and foresight—but alive like a tree. A tree that quietly exists, never moving except to sway in the wind, yet endlessly conversing with the sunlight and the soil. Using sunlight and water and nutrient minerals to grow and change. But all done so imperceptibly, that to me the old oak tree on the green is the same as it was when I was a child. ("Gaia: The Practical Science of Planetary Medicine", Gaia Books Limited, London, 1991, p.12.)

ORIGINS OF THE GAIAN METAPHOR

The actual term Gaia originates in a conversation with William Golding who suggested it to Lovelock as the name of the ancient Greek earth goddess - with all its mystical and quasi-religious connotations. James Lovelock appears to approve this religious connotation, whilst at the same time distancing himself from New Age philosophy and overemphasis on the goal-centred nature of Gaia as expressed in his early work. However, the idea of a living earth is ancient. Plato wrote:

> We shall affirm that the cosmos, more than anything else, resembles most closely that living Creature of which all other living creatures, severally or genetically, are portion; a living creature which is fairest of all and in ways most perfect.

Arguably we have only lost the understanding of Gaia, goddess and earth mother, the "world soul", the idea of "cosmic spirit" since the Enlightenment quest for objective science. In eastern philosophy it has never been lost. There were some advocates of a living earth even in the scientific period: James Hutton (earth as a super-organism, a physiological system), Humbolt and the (little known until recently) Russian scientist Vladimir Vernadsky, who introduced the concept of the biosphere.

Our conclusion here is that at least two models of Gaia have emerged in recent years: the model that life influences planetary processes (it has a substantial effect on abiotic processes) which has become known as the weak Gaia hypothesis. This model is widely supported. Secondly, there is Lovelock's original Gaia hypothesis, that life controls planetary processes (life created the Earth's system), has become known as the strong Gaia hypothesis. This is widely opposed.

SELF-REGULATING MECHANISMS

The essential idea of self-regulating **FEEDBACK LOOPS** is analogous therefore to the thermostat in your home. Here we consider four Gaian feedback mechanisms.

Mechanism 1 - Temperature maintained at + or -5°C.

Since life began on Earth, the energy provided by the Sun has increased by about 25% however, the surface temperature of the planet has only risen 5°C. How can it be that with such a warming of the sun, the earth's temperature has hardly risen?

Scientists have called this the **SNOWBALL EFFECT**. Lovelock has hypothesised that Dimethyl sulphide (**DMS**) was generated by this warming as an excretion of the biota (algae for example) which produced an effective heat shield. This caused much of this raised heat of the sun to bounce off cloud formations in the earth's atmosphere, providing a heat shield until such times as other gasses such as ozone were formed and took over the shielding role.

This is an example of a **NEGATIVE FEEDBACK LOOP** because the changes caused by the biota offset (negate) the shock effect of the positive warming of the sun. The question is: will the release of Greenhouse gasses following the industrial revolution upset the self-regulating mechanism within Gaia, so that Gaia takes revenge by wiping out or greatly reducing the human population (Lovelock has suggested, down to one billion from its present level of 7 billion)?

Mechanism 2 - Oxygen maintained at 21%

Oxygen needs to stay constant at 21% of the earth's atmosphere for biotic life to continue. The biota (for example, plants and trees) act as a giant recycling process, breathing in carbon dioxide and breathing out oxygen. The carbon residue gets locked up in the plants' cell structure, to be released as energy as humans burn fossil fuels. In the early period of Gaia's life, the role of greenhouse gasses such as **DMS** cooled the earth, but in the latter period it has warmed the earth so that the biggest periods of population increase have been caused by global warming.

PHOTOSYNTHESIS emerged in Gaia's history around 2.5 billion years ago and this accelerated the development of living species. The proportion of oxygen in the atmosphere has remained constant in this period at 21%. In the evolution of Gaia, photosynthesis was the key.

What would happen if oxygen were to reach, say, a proportion of 30% of the earth's atmosphere? Fires would occur whenever a lightening bolt hit forests. The planet would be in serious danger of burning up. What has kept oxygen from building up to dangerous levels? Why has it gone from nearly zero to 21%, and then stopped? One possible answer is the biological production of methane by bacteria. A short-lived molecule, methane might combine with oxygen to produce CO_2, thus stabilizing oxygen concentrations.

So Lovelock argues that Gaia regulates the physical and chemical environment of the planet to maintain suitable planetary conditions for the good of life itself. The planet can be thought of as a single, integrated, living entity with self-regulating abilities. This is the radical view that can be thought of as the "strong Gaia hypothesis".

Mechanism 3 - Ocean salinity maintained at 3.4%

Ocean salinity (salt concentration) has been constant at about 3.4% for a very long time. Stability of salt in ocean environments is important as most cells require a constant salinity and do not generally tolerate values above 5%. The reasons are mysterious, because river salts should have raised the ocean salinity much higher than the concentration we observe.

Mechanism 4 - Algae growth for carbon capture

Once the ocean temperature rises above 14°C it stratifies into layers of different water temperature, so the algae needs the temperature to be below 14 degrees to thrive. This natural cycle Lovelock describes as a 'small triumph of Gaia'. It is also an example of how Gaia itself may be producing a negative feedback loop (that is, one beneficial to life) in the face of global warming, mitigating the effects of the rise in man-made CO2.

Ocean algae are key agents in the recycling of carbon from its introduction to the atmosphere by volcanoes. Limestone rocks washed into the ocean combine with carbon as calcium bicarbonate which is used by algae to form shells which eventually fall to the sea floor to be buried, so locking away the excessive carbon dioxide. A gas is also released (dimethyl sulphide) which helps condensation in the atmosphere around which clouds form. Increased cloud cover reflects sunlight, so controlling surface temperature. There is some evidence that concentrations of ocean algal blooms are increasing. This may be a Gaian response to the present global warming.

These examples show how living beings have a major part to play in shaping the environment, through the creation and absorption of carbon dioxide and oxygen. But these are only four examples. All around us, plants and animals are recycling water, nutrients and gases in Earth's system in a complex process. In this vision of Gaia, it is difficult to accept the traditional scientific view of natural processes. Rather, Lovelock argues we should view the Earth as an organic whole, with properties that are observable on the vast scale of the atmosphere and the oceans.

Lovelock's conclusion is that:

> The Gaia hypothesis states that the lower atmosphere of the earth is an integral, regulated, and necessary part of life itself. For hundreds of millions of years, life has controlled the temperature, the chemical composition, the oxidising ability, and the acidity of the earth's atmosphere. (I.. Margulis and J. Lovelock, "Is Mars a Spaceship, Too?" Natural History, June/July 1976:86-90)

CRITIQUE OF GAIA

Criticism 1 - Gaia cannot be alive

Lovelock began by defining Gaia as a living organism, and later changed this to claims that it is a 'self-regulating system' (2006:166), and that the idea of Gaia as an organism was a metaphor.

> I am continuing to use the metaphor of the living earth for Gaia, but do not assume I am thinking of the Earth as alive in a sentient way, or even alive like an animal or bacterium. (2006:20)

According to his supporter the biologist Lynn Margulis, Lovelock initially defended the idea that "the earth is an organism" (2002:134) which she has never accepted: "I cannot stress strongly enough that Gaia is not a single organism" (1998:123), and in another book, "Rather than state "Earth is alive", we prefer to say that Gaia is a hypothesis about the planet Earth, its surface sediments, and its atmosphere" (1997:208).

Lovelock has backed away from the claim that Gaia is an organism but he also recognises the need for a definition of the concept 'life'. But he then ducks the issue by failing to give his own definition. He observes that the Dictionary of Biology has no entry for 'life'. In general biologists avoided the question, he says, but then reaffirms we should think of the planet 'as if it were alive' and 'keeping itself fit for life', 'like an animal' (2006:20-21). The idea of 'life' remains ambiguous.

Criticism 2 - Gaia cannot have a purpose

As late as 2006 Lovelock is still describing Gaia as a "goal-seeking entity that regulates itself on life's behalf" (2006:20). In his book The Extended Phenotype, Richard Dawkins criticises Lovelock's Gaia hypothesis for postulating that Gaia has a purpose over and above the Darwinian purpose of each of its elements - the self-interested function of promoting their own survival. There is no higher or larger purpose, according to Dawkins, either for entities themselves or the mythical idea of Gaia.

> If plants are supposed to make oxygen for the good of the biosphere, imagine a mutant plant which saved itself the costs of oxygen manufacture. Obviously it would outproduce its more public-spirited colleagues, and genes for public spiritedness would soon disappear. It is no use protesting that oxygen manufacture need not have costs: if it did not have costs, the most parsimonious explanation of oxygen production in plants would be the one the scientific world accepts anyway, that oxygen is a byproduct of something the plants do for their own selfish good. I do not deny that somebody may, one day, produce a workable model of the evolution of Gaia, although I personally doubt it. (1999:256)

Criticism 3 - Lovelock's response to Dawkins is unconvincing

Richard Dawkins rejected the implication of Gaia Theory – that it is Gaia herself (the living organism of Earth) that is doing the regulating, for the benefit of life as a whole. This view would seem to imply that Gaia has a **TELEOLOGICAL** purpose, while Dawkins considers nature as a "blind watchmaker'. Lovelock responded by developing a computer model called Daisyworld.

Daisyworld is a simplified planet which circles a sun whose output energy is ever-increasing. Scattered on Daisyworld are millions of seeds of the only two species found on the planet – black and white daisies.

Because of their colour, the black daisies are able to absorb the sun's energy more effectively than the white daisies, which reflect heat by the **ALBEDO EFFECT**. The black daisies spread because they are able to reproduce faster. The black daisies warm the atmosphere by absorbing energy, so making conditions more suitable for life in general. As the sun heats up further, white daisies begin to do better, since by reflecting heat they are able to avoid overheating. By reflecting the heat away from the planet, the white daisies also cool the planetary atmosphere.

Over a long period of time on Daisyworld, the temperature of the planet is automatically regulated by changes in the number of black and white daisies, competing according to the laws of Darwinian natural selection. So, Lovelock concludes, Gaian self-regulation can emerge automatically from a model, without needing to invoke teleological goals.

Critics point to the over-simplicity of the Daisyworld model, which they say can't tell us much about the vastly more complex real world.

Criticism 4 - Gaia is unscientific

Gaia has been accused of being unscientific in three senses:

1. It is based on inadequate data.

2. It is based on an anthropocentric metaphor, not a well-worked theory.

3. It is based on a teleological view of the earth, that the earth has a purpose, to sustain life, which is a fallacy.

We have considered the third criticism, posed by Richard Dawkins, in a previous section. But what of the other two?

The Gaia Hypothesis has since been tested by a number of scientific experiments. One of these is James Lovelock's Daisyworld model discussed above. It has also produced a number of useful predictions which allow some to make the claim that it is a scientific theory.

Moreover, the language of Gaia has become more widely accepted. In 2001, a thousand scientists at the European Geophysical Union meeting signed the Declaration of Amsterdam whose preamble states: "The Earth System behaves as a single, self-regulating system with physical, chemical, biological, and human components." The preamble seems to accept the starting point of Gaia, that the earth functions like one vast interdependent self-regulating organism.

However, a recent book by Professor Toby Tyrrell casts doubt on the scientific basis of Gaia. He writes:

> My aim was to determine whether the Gaia Hypothesis is a credible explanation of how life and environment interact on

Earth - I found it is not. Firstly, because there are no facts or phenomena that can be explained only by Gaia (no 'smoking gun'). Secondly, because there is no proven mechanism for Gaia (no accepted reason for why it should emerge out of natural selection). And thirdly, because the key lines of argument that Lovelock advanced in support of Gaia either give equally strong support to alternative hypotheses or else are mistaken.

Tyrell gives as an example the fact that, looking at the history of the planet, it has gone through fluctuations in climate some of which have proved very inhospitable for life. In its cold periods, the ice ages, there has been inadequate nitrogen to sustain life. In some periods of warming the ancestors of homo sapiens fell to just a few thousand people collected around the pole. Seawater chemical composition has also fluctuated widely. He prefers what he considers is a more powerful scientific argument which he calls **CO-EVOLUTION**.

Unlike Gaia, however, coevolution does not claim any emergent property out of the two-way interaction between life and environment. It is neutral with regards to predictions about the resulting effect on the environment. It does not suggest that the interaction tends to improve living conditions on Earth.

Clive Hamilton, a colleague of Tyrell, comments "There is no built-in stabiliser; life does not bring the planet back into equilibrium. Gaia is based on old science".

However, just as science has developed, so has James Lovelock's understanding of Gaia. He has modified his views significantly, abandoning much of the anthropocentric language and the views on in-built (teleological) purposes. The original hypothesis saw the Earth as a homeostatic system but that idea of homeostasis has itself been abandoned. Lovelock now admits that there is no equilibrium, only an indefinitely large range of quasi-stable states within a complex system. This is not the same thing as 'homeostasis.' Is a new consensus emerging?

HYPOTHESIS OR THEORY

Here is how, in two different emphases, Lovelock differentiates the Gaia hypothesis and the theory in the glossary to Revenge of Gaia (2007:208).

> *James Lovelock and Lynn Margulis postulated in the early 1970s that life on Earth actively keeps the surface conditions favourable for whatever is the contemporary ensemble of organisms. When introduced it was contrary to the conventional wisdom that life adapted to planetary conditions as it and they evolved in their separate ways. We now know that both the hypothesis as originally stated and the conventional wisdom were wrong. The hypothesis evolved into what is now Gaia Theory and the conventional wisdom into Earth System Science. (2007:208)*

> *Gaia theory is a view of the Earth that sees it as a self-regulating system made up from the totality of organisms, the surface rocks, the ocean and the atmosphere tightly coupled as an evolving system. The theory sees this system as having a goal— the regulation of surface conditions so as always to be as favourable as possible for contemporary life. It is based on observations and theoretical models; it is fruitful and has made ten successful predictions. (2007:208)*

In a book published in 2000, Ana Primaversi suggests a way forward which seems to chime with Tyrell's critique. She speaks of Gaia as:

> *The planet-sized system where the living and non-living components interact as two tightly coupled forces, each one shaping the other through systemic feedback loops. (2000:34)*

This, together with Tyrrell's recent book, does seem to suggest that a consensus is emerging over co-evolutionary Gaia, one of the weaker forms of the Gaia hypothesis which arguably is truer to Lovelock's recent writing. Coevolutionary coupling in these 'tightly coupled forces' implies that we are situated in a web of interdependent relations, and our place in this system has important implications for our ethics.

We could conclude that this regrading of Gaia from a 'hypothesis' to a 'theory' indicates a new role for Gaia as a quasi-scientific metaphor which poses questions, both physical and metaphysical, of humankind's relationship to the planet, and that Tyrell's critique may be part of an emerging consensus among scientists.

Meanwhile the metaphor of Gaia in process, striving with us and through us to make a better world, remains a source of inspiration and spiritual sustenance to many, a quasi-religious ideal.

Paul Taylor's Biocentrism

Taylor's biocentric egalitarianism claims to impute moral worth to all living things (the bios) in a way that escapes the charge of **ANTHROPOCENTRISM** (human-centredness) at the heart of many ethical theories. He argues for a deontological, duty-based ethics:

> *Environmental ethics is concerned with the moral relations that hold between humans and the natural world. The ethical principles governing those relations determine our duties, obligations, and responsibilities with regard to the Earth's natural environment and all animals and plants that inhabit it. (1986:3)*

Like Kantian ethics, then, Paul Taylor's is an ethic of **DUTY** and **RESPECT**. Indeed, the supreme moral value he seeks to establish, echoing the virtue ethics of Rosalind Hursthouse, is the virtue of **RESPECT FOR NATURE**. Human beings, using our enlightened reason, come to a kind of idealised view backed by a belief system acceptable to 'all those who are rational, factually informed, and have developed the capacity of reality-awareness' (1986:127). Yet, I would argue, his is an over-optimistic view which is ultimately flawed because it fails to create a convincing obligation to treat all living things with the respect, he argues, the natural world deserves.

Calling us to a new attitude, Taylor tries to give content to this 'respect for nature'. He writes:

Actions are right and character traits are morally good in virtue of their expressing or embodying a certain ultimate moral attitude, which I call respect for nature. (1986:84)

This an extension of the Kantian principle of respect for persons as ends in themselves. There is inherent worth in all living things which stems from our interdependence and their own **INTERESTS**. The interests consist in the fact that every living thing can be harmed or benefited - they have the ability to grow and develop and flourish according to their natures. He calls this a **POINT OF VIEW**, although we must stress that all living things can have a 'point of view' whether conscious or not.

Taylor distinguishes himself from Leopold by stressing that his theory is not fundamentally holistic.

COMPONENTS OF A BIOCENTRIC OUTLOOK

Taylor suggests four main components of the outlook of 'respect for nature':

1. Humans are merely members of the biotic community.

We have no privileged position, indeed, according to Taylor we arrived late on the scene. Also, as animals, we are entirely dependent on the ecological system for survival: 'while they can do without us, we cannot do without them', he argues. Humans might even be seen as nasty pests, with nothing but good consequences for the rest of Earth's living things if we died out: "from a certain perspective, the preservation of the human species may not be a good. It cannot just be assumed without question." (1986:99)

2. All ecosystems are built up of a web of interconnected and interdependent organisms.

The long term ecological equilibrium is necessary for the continued existence of all individual living things. This holistic nature of ecosystems, though, is a factual aspect of the Earth, and does not lead automatically to any moral values.

3. Each individual living thing is "conceived of as a teleological centre of life".

This means it has its own goals and its own "biological function".

We conceive of the organism as a teleological centre of life, striving to preserve itself and realise its good in its own unique way. To say it is a teleological centre of life is to say that its internal functioning as well as its external activities are all goal-oriented, having the constant tendency to maintain the organism's existence through time and to enable it successfully to perform those biological operations. (1986:121)

Even inanimate plants can have a point of view and a **TELEOLOGICAL CENTRE OF LIFE**, striving to 'achieve their goals' and 'what is good or bad for it can be understood by reference to its own survival, health, and well-being. As a living thing it seeks its own ends in a way', (1986:125).

4. Humans are not in any way superior to other living things.

Humans must give up their arrogance towards other living things, because we have 'disordered nature'. There is no reason to think that our special capabilities are somehow superior to any other organism's special attributes and capabilities. To do so reminds us of the hierarchical class structure artificially imposed throughout human history. Nor is there any reason to think that we are superior, as in the religious viewpoint, just because we possess a soul.

It was the same order of evolutionary processes, governed by the same laws of natural selection and genetic transmission, that gave rise to our existence and to the existence of every other species. (1986:110)

Whether we ought to survive depends, according to Taylor, whether we are prepared to play a sympathetic role as equal partners of an interdependent ecosphere, dedicated to fulfilling our obligations to each of its parts.

FOUR NEW DUTIES

Kantian ethics is fundamentally anthropocentric (human-centred) with a emphasis on autonomy, reason and 'respect for persons'. Taylor widens the idea of respect in his biocentric ethic to include 'respect for nature'. However, Taylor's ethic shares with Kant a number of features, because the moral good must be formulated as general laws which apply universally to all human beings as moral agents - Kant's principle of universalisability. As with Kant, human beings take an imaginative step backwards out of a situation and look at all the interests involved, asking the question, 'what would the world and the environment be like if everyone behaved like this'?

All wild animals and plants have inherent worth as members of the biotic community of a natural ecosystem. They are **MORAL SUBJECTS** to which duties are owed by **MORAL AGENTS**. It's here that Taylor goes beyond Kantian ethics and states:

> *Whatever its species may be, none is thought to be superior to another and all are held to be deserving of equal consideration. (1968:79)*

Such an egalitarian, biocentric position should be accepted, he insists, and to be moral we need to adopt the point of view of each living thing.

What rules do we derive from our human reason, applying this biocentric point of view, and including all creatures and plants within the biosphere? There are four basic duties according to Taylor.

1. **NONMALIFIENCE** - Humans as moral agents have the duty not to do any harm to any entity in the natural environment that has a good of its own.

2. **NONINTERFERENCE** - Humans have two negative obligations : to refrain from placing restrictions on the freedom of an individual, and the second, not to interfere with ecosystems and biotic communities.

3. **FIDELITY** - Humans have the duty not to break the trust that a wild animal places in us (as often done in hunting, trapping and fishing).

4. **RESTITUTIVE JUSTICE** - We share the duty to restore the balance of justice between a moral agent and a moral subject when the subject has been wronged.

Sometimes moral conflicts emerge between human rights and the good of nonhuman life. Therefore Taylor proposes a set of additional principles governed by **FAIRNESS**: all parties to the conflict are to be treated fairly. There are five such conflict-resolving 'priority principles':

1. **SELF DEFENCE** - It is permissible for moral agents to protect themselves against dangerous or harmful organisms (or animals) by destroying them (think here of the Ebola crisis of 2014 and the suffering in West Africa caused by this deadly virus).

2. **PROPORTIONALITY** - Greater weight is given to basic than to nonbasic interests, no matter what species, human or otherwise. A basic interest might include self-preservation and the right to life.

3. **MINIMUM WRONG** - When humans feel they must violate nonhuman interests, they should act in the way which causes least harm.

4. **DISTRIBUTIVE JUSTICE** - This requires that when the interests of the parties are all basic ones and there exists a natural source of good, each party must be given an equal share. For example, an area of wild country where animals graze but which is also pastureland for flocks of domestic animals.

5. **RESTITUTIVE JUSTICE** - Some form of pay back or compensation is needed. For example, the general practice of creating National Parks and World heritage sites for special protection is a matter of fairness to wild animals and plants.

When the principles are followed Taylor believes we can move towards the greatest good (the summum bonum of Kantian ethics) which embraces the needs and interests of both human beings and the biotic community of animals, plants and other living species. To do this we must abandon the belief in the superiority of our own interests and embrace equality (hence 'biocentric egalitarianism').

EVALUATING TAYLOR

1. **THE PROBLEM OF EQUALITY** - Egalitarianism as an ideal sounds fine, but lacks practical force. Moreover, if it means treating species that are in fact unequal, equally (a rat and a human being for example) then it results in a moral wrong, that of injustice to the human species. It is unclear what it means to attribute equality to things a divergent as a weed, a rat, a chimpanzee and a human being.

2. **THE PROBLEM OF CONFLICTING INTERESTS** - If a tree has interests and so do the people whose housing estate is being built on a parcel of woodland, then two sets of interests conflict. Where there is conflict it is not sufficient to argue that 'we are interdependent and trees have inherent worth'. Worth of what sort? Every species of tree and bush? And how are we to judge between the interests of both?

3. **THE PROBLEM OF INHERENT WORTH** - Taylor emphasises that nature has 'inherent worth' particularly that part of it that experiences life (whether conscious or not is apparently irrelevant). Yet if we abandon the anthropocentric (human-based) outlook, then how is this worth assessed? For example it is easy to impute worth to something if it serves human interests (crops, farm animals, the rainforest). But if we take away this perspective, what about viruses, weeds, and predators that take our animals? But to impute worth to interests begs the question - it may be in the virus' interest to inhabit my body, but is that 'good'?

4. **THE PROBLEM OF ADOPTING A POINT OF VIEW** - Lyzsak Pyra notes "Taylor claims that it is possible for a human being to

take an animal's standpoint without the slightest trace of anthropomorphism. I cannot agree with such an opinion; although it is possible for man to make rather informed, objective judgements what is desirable and undesirable for a nonhuman living being, the problem is that a human being can only vaguely, I think, approach the animal's standpoint. The author, unfortunately, goes even further when he claims the same to be true about plants".

My conclusion is that Taylor has side-stepped the problem of intrinsic value mentioned in the opening chapter, and failed ultimately to make a convincing case for his ideas of inherent worth. His ethic lacks practical force because it fails to solve the problem of competing interests (despite giving us a number of priority principles) which lies at the heart of the study of ethics. His ethic continues to be framed as one rational human viewpoint which lacks adequate grounds for collective commitment. It fails, in other words, to answer the question 'why should I be moral' when the benefit to my own species is not clearcut.

Five Ethical Theories and Environmental Ethics

Traditional ethical theories have generally been criticised for being **ANTHROPOCENTRIC** - basing the idea of moral value on human rights, or human happiness, or human rationality. In recent years, led for example by Peter Singer's work on Animal Liberation, there has been a reappraisal of the relationship between orthodox theories and environmental ethics. In this chapter I will contrast the old and new interpretations and try to explain why we need to be careful before dismissing traditional theories of ethics as harmful to the cause of environmental preservation.

KANTIAN ETHICS

In recent years modern Kantians such as Allen Wood and Christine Korsgaard have sought to bring to our attention passages in Kant which are more sympathetic to the environmental cause. The key question seems to be which of the various formulations of the categorical imperative do we take as our starting point, and how do we apply these to inanimate things and to sentient beings?

Interpretation 1 - Kant ignores the environment

The first interpretation takes as its starting point the principle of autonomy. Human beings are free, autonomous, self-legislating beings who make the moral law by an imaginative step away from any individual situation into an a priori state in which we universalise our behaviour. In Kant's lectures on anthropology, for example, he explains:

> The fact that a human being can have the representation 'I' raises him infinitely above all the other beings on earth. By this he is a person, being altogether different in rank and dignity from things, such as irrational animals, with which one may deal and dispose at one's discretion. (VA 7:127)

Human beings have a unique status and dignity because of our rational natures. According to Kant 'this raises us infinitely above' other sentient beings. We become not just moral subjects (the subjects of the moral law) but moral agents (we think and act to create the moral law and our choices define who we are).

In a different essay Kant explains how a gulf opens up between human beings and the rest of nature. Human beings realised that they had dominion over the animal kingdom because our intellects made us superior beings placing animals 'at the disposal of our will'.

> The first time a human being said to the sheep, 'Nature gave the skin you wear not for you but for me', and then took it off the sheep and put it on himself (Genesis 3:21), he became aware of the prerogative he had by nature over all animals, which he no longer saw as fellow creatures, but as means and tools at the disposal of his will for the attainment of the aims of his own discretion. (MA 8:114)

The principle of universalisability gives us direct duties of respect and of love to our fellow human beings, so to act as the principle created by universalising our own behaviour dictates. It gives us no direct duties over non-rational animals or the wider environment who do not share our rational dignity.

However, Kant is surprisingly modern in his stand against animal cruelty. Kant thinks it is permissible to kill animals for human ends (such as for food); but he insists that this should be done as painlessly as possible (MS 6:443). Killing animals for sport is morally wrong (VE 27:460). Kant describes as morally abominable "agonizing physical experiments on animals, carried out for the sake of mere speculation, or whose end can be achieved in other ways" (MS 6:443).

Interpretation 2: We have indirect duties to nature

In Kantian ethics an indirect duty exists when any duties we owe to animals are in fact duties owed to humans. Indirect duties may be derived from the second formulation of the categorical imperative, the formula of ends: 'so act that you use humanity, whether in your own person or in the person of any other, always at the same time as an end, never merely as a means'.(G 4:429.)

Christine Korsgaard points out two elements to this principle. First of all, we don't use people. People aren't simply a means to our own pleasure or happiness. But secondly, we also pay attention to our own ends as 'good and worthy of pursuit' (Tanner Lecture). We are also committed to pass moral laws in a kind of spiritual community of rational, equal beings, which Kant calls the 'kingdom of ends', in which we assign value to whatsoever we choose.

Not everything Kant says about the formula of ends is favourable to nature. "Beings ... without reason, have only a relative worth, as means, and are therefore called things, whereas rational beings are called persons because their nature ... marks them out as an end in itself". But Korsgaard points us to other passages which create stronger indirect duties towards animals.

> *Violent and cruel treatment of animals is ... intimately opposed to a human being's duty to himself...; for it dulls his shared feeling of their suffering and so weakens and gradually uproots a natural disposition that is very serviceable to morality in one's relations with other people.*

For example there may be a link between animal cruelty and domestic abuse or other forms of violent behaviour. Kant is arguing that being cruel to non-human animals makes us more likely to be cruel to humans, and that is what makes animal cruelty wrong. The animal itself doesn't matter for its own sake as an end-in-itself in this argument. If cruelty to animals made individuals less likely to harm other humans, then Kant would have had to conclude that being cruel to animals was therefore good.

So these indirect duties exist to promote our own moral perfection by behaving in ways that encourage in us a morally good attitude and character. Being kind to animals helps create sympathy and love towards our fellow human beings, whilst cruelty toward animals promotes the contrary vices, and so makes worse people of us.

These indirect duties build our own moral perfection. The natural world and animal life is therefore protected (in this indirect way) by the principle of ends, because in treating them as ends in themselves we learn to treat others with dignity and respect and so establish the greater moral good.

THE NATURAL MORAL LAW

Natural Law theory, derived from Aristotle and developed by Aquinas, has been adopted as the official moral standpoint of the Roman Catholic Church. It sees goodness related to our ultimate purposes, and at the heart of Natural Law ethics is a concept of well-being (Greek: **EUDAIMONIA**). But how wide do we cast the net? Do we include the welfare of animals and plants, for example? Is the world seen as fundamentally hierarchical, a pyramid of life with humans at the top? Or is it seen as holistic with interdependent parts seeking their own individual perfection?

Here I again contrast two interpretations and argue that the traditional view of Natural Law as ignoring or even abusing the environment for human ends not the only reading of the theory. Moreover, in recent years the Roman Catholic interpretation of Natural Law has increasingly embraced environmental concerns. This implies a view of practical rationality where reasonable behaviour is grounded on well-being (Murphy 2001,100) and basic goods include life, knowledge, aesthetic experience, excellence in play and work, inner peace, friendship and community, religion and happiness. Natural things flourish by fulfilling their function just as human beings flourish by fulfilling their function.

Interpretation 1 - a hierarchy with man at the top

Aristotle argued that for every living thing there was a function and purpose. This is a **TELEOLOGICAL** worldview, where we go beyond simple biology (the examination of how things work) to ask the question why things work like that. Why are human beings endowed with reason? Why does a plant turn towards the sun? Goodness is linked to function, and function to cause. There are four causes of an object or a living being, according to Aristotle:

1. Material - its matter

2. Formal - how matter is organised

3. Efficient - how something comes to be

4. Final - the purpose or characteristic of the object.

Aristotle thought that we do not understand an object until we understand its final cause or telos (purpose), but there is a common goal for all things. He calls this goal eudaimonia, or personal and social flourishing and well-being. To attain our ultimate well-being we must align our life to our natural activity. This soul or life-force he calls the **PSYCHE** and it is its presence linked to its function that defines whether something is alive. As Des Jardins notes 'the good of any living thing is to attain its natural activity, the good of the soul" (2000:28) Aristotle describes three powers or functions of the psyche:

• Nutritive - plants reproduce themselves and grow

• Appetitive - animals possess appetites

• Deliberative - only humans possess this function uniquely

Thus plants can fulfil their telos by growing and reproducing, animals by growing reproducing and satisfying their appetites, humans by these attributes as well as thinking and leading a deliberative life. Des Jardins concludes: "only humans possess the three life activities of nutrition, appetite and thought." (2000:28). The problem for Natural Law ethics and the environment comes when we interpret the additional deliberative functions of human beings as implying superiority. In a number of passages Aristotle implies that animals exist for our sake:

> *Plants exist for the sake of animals...all other animals exist for the sake of man, tame animals for the use he can make of them as well as for the food they provide; and as for wild animals, most though not all of these can be used for food and are useful in other ways; clothing and tools can be made out of them. If then we are right in believing that nature makes nothing without some end in view, nothing to no purpose, it must be that nature has made all things specifically for the sake of man. (Politics, Book 1)*

Aquinas accepted, and modified, Aristotle's hierarchy. In a long passage in Summa Theologica Aquinas asks whether it is lawful to kill living things. The answer seems to be an unqualified 'yes'. Plants are less perfect than animals and animals less perfect than human beings. This divine order is designed into the world as part of God's gift to superior man.

> *There is no sin in using a thing for the purpose for which it is. Now the order of things is such that the imperfect are for the perfect, even as in the process of generation nature proceeds from imperfection to perfection. Hence it is that just as in the generation of a man there is first a living thing, then an animal, and lastly a man, so too things, like the plants, which merely have life, are all alike for animals, and all animals are for man. Wherefore it is not unlawful if man use plants for the good of animals, and animals for the good of man, as the Philosopher states (Polit. i, 3).*

Now the most necessary use would seem to consist in the fact that animals use plants, and men use animals, for food, and this cannot be done unless these be deprived of life: wherefore it is lawful both to take life from plants for the use of animals, and from animals for the use of men. On fact this is in keeping with the commandment of God Himself: for it is written (Genesis 1:29-30): "Behold I have given you every herb . . . and all trees . . . to be your meat, and to all beasts of the earth": and again (Genesis 9:3): "Everything that moves and lives shall be meat to you." (ST II II Q64 A1)

Interpretation 2 - the eternal law sees ultimate goodness in our interdependence

Aquinas identifies four forms of law. Human law is the law we work out in human society; the divine law is revealed to us in the written form of the Bible; natural law is worked out as our reason pays attention to the proper ends and purposes of human life.

However, there is a law that is fundamental to the holistic nature of our Universe. This is called the **ETERNAL LAW** - a kind of blueprint in the mind of God which explains the complex interdependency of our planet. In fact Aquinas raises the question "whether the image of God is to be found in irrational creatures?" (ST II II Q93, A2). He then explicitly disagrees with the view that Divine Goodness is found in rational creatures alone. The whole universe is in the image of God, and 'all things together are called very good'.

The more perfect anything is in goodness, the more it is like God. But the whole universe is more perfect in goodness than man; for though each individual thing is good, all things together are called very good. Therefore the whole universe is to the image of God, and not only man. (ST II II Q93 A2)

As Willis Jenkins notes 'God desires that creation's perfection unfold through a plenitude of singular perfections related to one another through the complex good of the universe'. (Ecologies of Grace, page 123) Even a swallow fulfils its part in the perfection of God's order participating in the eternal law in a way that is unique to it. And God calls upon ravens to act as ravens, not to sing like angels. Thomas' vision is therefore one of the integrity, the wholeness of creation with each part playing its role according to its own perfection.

By tending to emphasise natural law, we have been in danger of cutting humans off from the context in which we live. So papal encyclicals (such as Veritatis Splendor, 1995) have paid inadequate attention to the idea of the perfection of nature - the created world seen as 'very good' in God's eternal plan.

But as climate change and the extinction of species accelerates, it has become all too clear that a divine blueprint of the created world cannot include this speed and extent of degradation. The very scale and time period becomes a moral issue. Moreover, we can observe its effects in, for instance, the huge north Pacific whirl-pool of plastic bags and debris the size of Texas which circles just north of Hawaii. Respect for nature becomes an extension of a shared moral respect for the dignity of human beings.

This view is echoed by Pope Benedict: "respect for the human being and respect for nature are one and the same, but they will both be able to develop and to reach their full dimension if we respect the Creator and his creature in the human being and in nature," (Benedict, 2011). But even in a revised form of Natural Law, human beings are still essentially at the top of a pyramid of creation.

Roman Catholic interpretation of Natural Law

The Roman Catholic Church has tended to take an anthropocentric view of the environment, emphasising humankind's role as a responsible steward at the pinnacle of creation. Moreover, Veritatis Splendor, the papal encyclical of 1995, indicates that the Church takes Aquinas' primary precepts as their starting point. These precepts set the goals in broad terms which rational persons will pursue to fulfil their God-given nature.

> Precisely because of this "truth" the natural law involves universality. Inasmuch as it is inscribed in the rational nature of the person, it makes itself felt to all beings endowed with reason and living in history. In order to perfect himself in his specific order, the person must do good and avoid evil, be concerned for the transmission and preservation of life, refine and develop the riches of the material world, cultivate social life, seek truth, practise good and contemplate beauty. (VS, 1995:51)

A number of things are surprising about this paragraph. There is a clear reference to Aquinas' **SYNDERESIS** principle, that we by nature 'do good and avoid evil'. The precept 'worship of God' has been changed to 'appreciation of beauty' in line with modern Natural Law theory which tends to stress 'aesthetic appreciation' (Murphy, 2001). But what really surprises us is the weakness of the environmental statement that to perfect ourselves we are to 'refine and develop the riches of the material world', which sounds like a licence to exploit and commercialise natural resources for the good of human beings. This weak environmentalism, not surprisingly, has failed to motivate Catholics into the sort of lifestyle changes that Caritas in Veritate, a later encyclical from 2009, exhorts us to adopt:

> *The way humanity treats the environment influences the way it treats itself, and vice versa. This invites contemporary society to a serious review of its life-style, which, in many parts of the world, is prone to hedonism and consumerism, regardless of their harmful consequences. What is needed is an effective shift in mentality which can lead to the adoption of new life-styles "in which the quest for truth, beauty, goodness and communion with others for the sake of common growth are the factors which determine consumer choices, savings and investments. (CV, 2009: 51)*

Conclusion

Natural Law theory can be adapted to include an environmental ethic, even if there is validity in the accusation that Aquinas' formulation of Natural Law envisages a pyramid of creation with human beings at the top. I have argued here, however, that within Aquinas' writing there are also hints of a holistic theory of the environment, which sees the whole of the natural world as one interdependent creation with the perfection of each species as a key to fulfilling God's ultimate purpose of perfection of the cosmos (Aristotle's **EUDAIMONIA**).

There are two further interpretations of Natural Law, one emphasising the place of primary precepts and the other, the source of the Eternal Law. The Catholic Church has adapted the concept of primary precepts and included, as an extension of preservation of life, a weak environmental ethic which falls short of attributing to the natural world any idea of intrinsic goodness. The closest they get is in one sentence in Caritas in Veritate which speaks of 'respecting the intrinsic balance of creation' (2009:51).

It is to be hoped that Pope Francis in a new encyclical to be published shortly will address this problem. One way forward is to develop Aquinas' four laws and to take as a fundamental starting point the idea of the Eternal Law. This richer concept may yet lift Catholic environmentalism above the charge of anthropocentrism and help to bring about the shift in lifestyles that previous Catholic documents have called us to adopt.

UTILITARIANISM

Utilitarianism is a theory of **INTRINSIC GOODNESS** which seeks to maximise the greatest happiness for the greatest (whether of people or of sentient beings depends which version we take). There is only one absolute, non-negotiable intrinsic good, pleasure or happiness which is then assessed according to an **EMPIRICAL** calculation of consequences (past or future). Here we consider three variations of utilitarian ethics, the pleasure-based **ACT UTILITARIAN** theory of Jeremy Bentham, the rights and virtue-based **RULE** utilitarianism of Mill and the **PREFERENCE** and interest-based theory of Peter Singer. All three theories are anthropocentric because moral value is linked to human happiness and welfare, and decisions are assessed according to the likely consequences of human behaviour in maximising pleasure and minimising pain.

However, in two ways we can see that utilitarian ethics strengthens the case for caring for the environment:

1. By introducing the idea that all **SENTIENT** (feeling) beings share in the moral calculation of good and bad, because they feel pleasure and they feel pain. So utilitarian ethics in all three forms has been strong on animal rights, linking rights to **INTERESTS**.

2. By leaving open-ended how human beings see their own happiness and welfare, utilitarians open up the possibility that environmental protection might be considered a top priority in our own moral calculation - that the effects of, say, climate change, may be seen by many to be so painful that radical moral action is seen to be desirable and indeed, obligatory.

Bentham - sentience is what counts - of all species

In the eighteenth century the view that only humans count was challenged by the utilitarian Jeremy Bentham. Bentham argued that only pleasure was intrinsically good, and it didn't matter what the quality of pleasure was, only its quantity. There was no difference between a higher order primate like a human being listening to and enjoying Mozart, and a lioness enjoying a good chase and meal of a water buffalo. In making moral decisions, therefore, we have to consider all creatures, rational or not, that have the capacity to experience pleasure or pain.

Bentham was a radical social reformer who saw all human begins as strictly equal. He famously declared that 'everyone is to count as one, and no-one as more than one', meaning that the Queen and a poor farmer had an equal number of hedon-votes in his moral democracy. At a time when slavery, transportation of prisoners to colonies, and the death penalty were widely used, Bentham praised the French for liberating slaves:

> The day may come when the rest of the animal creation may acquire those rights which never could have been withholden from them but by the hand of tyranny. The French have already discovered that the blackness of the skin is no reason why a human being should be abandoned without redress to the caprice of a tormentor.

Using a **HEDONIC CALCULUS** Bentham believed we could attach hedons (a measure of the value of pleasure) to different choices and then add up the total pleasure of an action. We can also take away the value of the pain so caused to other human beings to give us the net welfare or net pleasure of an action. But Bentham extended his theory to all sentient (feeling) beings. He argued that it was illogical to give special status to humans because of our cognitive ability, as,

> A full-grown horse or dog is beyond comparison a more rational, as well as a more conversable animal, than an infant of a day, or a week, or even a month old. The question is not, Can they reason nor Can they talk, but, Can they suffer?

Bentham set the scene for the development of the "animal rights" movement. For humans to fail to recognise the moral standing of animals, utilitarians argued, is discrimination on the basis of species, which is as morally wrong as discrimination on the basis of race or sex.

Mill - justice is what counts - for all species

In an early essay Mill called it a 'superstition of selfishness' to suppose that the suffering of animals was of no moral importance. Because animals are sentient beings, they are capable of being harmed and therefore come under the **HARM PRINCIPLE** discussed in Mill's essay On Liberty.

In that essay Mill argues for 'one very simple principle' that:

> The only purpose for which power can be rightfully exercised over any other member of a civilised community, against his will, is to prevent harm to others.

Mill then extends the harm principle to all sentient beings. In a chapter on the 'Limits of the Province of Government' in the Principles of Political

Economy of 1848, he argues that 'ruffianism', the wilful cruelty to animals, should be made illegal:

> The reasons for legal intervention in favour of mistreated children, apply not less strongly to the case of these unfortunate slaves and victims of the most brutal part of mankind, the lower animals. It is by the grossest misunderstanding of the principles of liberty, that the infliction of exemplary punishment on ruffianism practised towards these defenceless creatures has been treated as a meddling by government with things beyond its province.

Mill's 'harm principle' therefore rules out forcing people to act as other people think they should act, except where their actions are liable to cause others harm. These harms include pain to all feeling beings. To Mill it is morally wrong to torture, bait, mistreat enslave or even kill an animal. Mill extended this to hunting, which he believe should be banned: in a letter he praised the views of a historian Edward Freeman:

> I honour him for having broken ground against field sports, a thing I have often been tempted to do myself, but having so many unpopular causes already on my hands, thought it wiser not to provoke fresh hostility.

Singer - interests are what counts - of all species

In his book Animal Liberation Peter Singer poses us with a challenge: if possessing a higher degree of intelligence does not entitle us to use another for our own ends, how can it entitle humans to exploit nonhumans for the same purpose? In other words, he suggests that having higher cognitive faculties is not a significant moral difference, for if it was, it would allow me to use other human begins for my own ends who were less able, or intelligent, than myself. So the only relevant fact is whether a being is sentient and can feel pain:

> *The capacity for suffering and enjoyment is, however, not only necessary, but also sufficient for us to say that a being has interests - at an absolute minimum, an interest in not suffering. A mouse, for example, does have an interest in not being kicked along the road because it will suffer if it is. (1975:8)*

Singer introduces the idea of interests which sits uneasily alongside his preference utilitarianism. Preferences need to be stated, and to express a preference I need to be conscious, have self-understanding and some ability to communicate. But newly born infants, animals and this with disabilities have difficulty expressing preferences. But clearly they still have interests. Animals have an objective benefit relative to their own species - those conditions which cause the animal to flourish, and so, Singer argues:

> *The limit of sentience is the only defensible boundary of concern for the interests of others. To mark this boundary by some other characteristic like intelligence or rationality would be to mark it in an arbitrary manner. Why not choose some other characteristic, like skin colour?*

So Singer, calls on fellow humanists to take a strong moral stand against cruelty to animals. To fail to act is to be guilty of **SPECIESISM**, placing our species above other species as a form of prejudice as morally serious as racism or sexism. On his website Singer urges:

It is time for humanists to take a stand against this ruthless exploitation of other sentient beings, which is so powerfully buttressed by the religious view that human beings are God's special creation and that he gave them dominion over animals.... despite many individual exceptions, humanists have on the whole been unable to free themselves from one of the most central of these Christian dogmas: the prejudice of speciesism.

Problems with the utilitarian view

1. **THE PROBLEM OF INHERENT VALUE -** Tom Regan argues that Utilitarians are always instrumental in their idea of goodness; something is good as a means to human happiness or pleasure. We grant value to the natural world (or fail to give it value). Even Singer's idea of interests relies on human beings to interpret and define those interests (clearly animals can't do that for themselves). Regan wants to replace this idea of instrumental value with the "Postulate of Inherent Value": individuals have value independently of their experience and their value to others. He rejects idea that value comes in measurable degrees and higher beings have more perfections and lesser beings have more imperfections. Regan argues: "Individuals are subjects of a life if they have beliefs and desires; perception, memory and a sense of the future, including their own future; an emotional life together with feelings of pleasure and pain; preference and welfare interest; the ability to initiate action in pursuit of their desires and goals; a Psychophysical identity over time; and an individual welfare in the sense that their experiential life fare well or ill for them, logically independently of their utility to others," (2004:243). However, when those who aspire to extend

this idea of inherent value to inanimate nature (a rock or a tree) then they 'certainly have their work cut out' for them (2004:247).

2. **THE PROBLEM OF CALCULATION** - We cannot know how other animals feel. Singer replies, we cannot know generally what other people feel either, and so we need to try to take a universal viewpoint and imagine how they are likely to feel, given their circumstances.

3. **THE PROBLEM OF NATURALISM** - Utilitarians are naturalists. They argue that pleasure and pain are natural features of the world, to be desired for their own sake. Moral principles are human creations which we impose on the natural world - we move from a naturalistic observation 'animals feel pain' to a moral obligation 'we ought not to inflict pain on animals'. Can we make this leap?

4. **THE PROBLEM OF ANIMAL CRUELTY** - Cats play with mice; magpies kill sparrows; foxes slaughter the whole chicken-house; films show a pride of lions cornering a water buffalo and subjecting it to a long slow death. Should animals be restrained from torturing other animals?

5. **THE PROBLEM OF UNBORN GENERATIONS** - According to climate change pessimists, global warming of + 2 degrees centigrade will happen within 100 years and cause a catastrophic rise in sea levels, desertification of swathes of central Africa, food shortages, migration and disease. But how many people will be affected? And how do we weigh the interests of those unborn against the interest of people alive today who require economic growth to raise them out of poverty?

Conclusion - two interpretations

My argument here has been, that with moral theories there is often more than one way of constructing an argument. This is true of the question 'can utilitarian ethic produce a defensible ethic of the environment'? In this section I have concentrated on the interesting question of animal rights - but environmental ethics asks us to go further than that and consider the interest of the planet in an age of pollution, exploitation of resources and climate change. Here are two arguments.

▸ **Interpretation 1 - utilitarianism is fatally compromised by its anthropocentrism**

According to this line of argument, humans are the source of the utilitarian value-system because goodness is seen from the standpoint of human happiness. Humans define the value and also make the calculation. It is also human choices which ultimately have consequences for the whole planet, as animals and other sentient beings do not make moral choices for which we hold them responsible. Because utilitarians take a **SHORT-TERM** view, these consequences are assessed only in terms of immediate satisfaction or dissatisfaction. Human beings cannot long postpone consumption, and for many (those who are starving for example) the idea of not polluting, or not building a power station is an irrelevant moral choice. Self-preservation trumps everything else. Preservation of the planet means sacrifices have to be made - things cost more, trees aren't cut down the rainforest is protected, the loggers are banned. But hedonistic utilitarians will not make this sacrifice.

More seriously, rich nations are accused of moral hypocrisy. China argues, with some justification, that when carbon emissions per head in China match those of the United States, then they will stop building coal-fired power stations which add to global warming. Meantime, the USA fails to sign up to the Koyoto Agreement to curb carbon emissions, pursues a policy of low energy prices and is reluctant to pass laws that impose costs on business. They take, in other words, a narrow selfish view of happiness which fails JS Mill's test of caring for others, whereby human beings have the virtue of sympathy for strangers which causes them to act altruistically and make sacrifices for the environmental good. The cost to those in developed countries doesn't appear to match the benefit. It is a utilitarian failure, born of short-termism.

▶ Interpretation 2 - utilitarianism can give inherent worth to the environment for general welfare reasons

An alternative argument would take as its starting point Mill's version of utilitarian ethics. Mill argued that social virtues were required to build the idea of the common good. General happiness is best served by generally following rules which are based on the past experience of wise people who have reflected on the welfare-maximising choice. The key virtue here is sympathy: we care for others, argues Mill, because we feel pleasure with them and we also feel their pain, so that our own self-interest is swallowed up in a communal interest.

Mill would argue today for the strengthening of these social rules that govern human behaviour. He would see education as the key to building a happier future because through education we can see the effect of our behaviour on future populations. We can sympathise with those yet unborn. Moreover, young people can cause behaviour changes in the elderly (for example, witness the attitude to smoking cigarettes taken by the younger generation today).

This chimes well with Mill's qualitative view of pleasure. Those who have been taught to appreciate and experience both the higher aesthetic pleasure of a beautiful, unpolluted world, and to feel the pain of seeing species vanish, floods become more frequent, or famine break out in Africa will act responsibly and change their behaviour. For Mill, moral virtues (a concern for truth, justice and sympathy for others) boost the utilitarian case. But this requires us to value the higher pleasures, and build social norms that are reflected in rules, and to despise the lower pleasures that lead to over-consumption and self-gratification.

In this way rule utilitarianism gives us hope for a future in which human beings escape narrow self-interest and truly work for the common good.

VIRTUE ETHICS

Virtues express themselves in what virtuous people do, and vices in what virtuous people avoid doing. This may sound like a tautology, but not when it is linked to the ultimate goal or **TELOS** of the flourishing individual the flourishing society and the flourishing world.

We would therefore expect virtues to reflect themselves in virtuous activity, but the nature of that activity to be contextual. In other words it depends on the context (what Alasdair MacIntyre calls a 'form of life' in After Virtue) what virtue we apply and what practical action we take. This is the decision of **PHRONESIS** or practical wisdom. Not only does this determine which virtue we identify as important, but it enables us to determine new virtues when faced with new issues. This, argues Rosalind Hursthouse, is exactly what is required when we face the issues produced by climate change, or the use of agrochemicals on crops (to take two examples).

The use of agrochemicals can be taken to illustrate how virtues and practical action go together. If in Argentina it can be established that the spraying of agrochemicals on soya crops is producing cancers in children and miscarriages in pregnant women, then the virtuous person would act to prevent these things happening under the virtue of care and compassion. But go one stage back and we discover chemical companies protesting that "we take the welfare of our communities very seriously". They are arguing for the virtue of care. However, what are they doing to prove that they care in the practice of this virtue?

We suspect (perhaps cynically) that in business interests such as the desire for profit come in the way of the virtues. So we would ask whether these same companies are spending money to research the high incidence of cancers among children. After all, if there is a link, it must be proved. But if these same companies are spending no money on such research even in the presence of statistical anomaly of high cancer rates, we would accuse them, quite rightly, of having the vice of indifference. We would say, objectively speaking, that they do not care.

The question therefore arises: why should we care about the environment, and how, if we can establish that carelessness will produce the destruction of the planet and hence the end of the human race (an extreme form of lack of flourishing), then what virtues do we need to make sure such defects are addressed?

It is here that Rosalind Hursthouse (2006) acknowledges an indebtedness to the environmentalist Paul Taylor. Taylor introduces an idea which we could ascribe as a virtue, the value of 'respect for nature'.

> One sees one's membership in the Earth's Community of Life as providing a common bond with all the different species of animals and plants that have evolved over the ages. One becomes aware that, like all other living things on our planet, one's very existence depends on the fundamental soundness and integrity of the biological system of nature. When one looks at this domain of life in its totality, one sees it to be a complex and unified web of interdependent parts. (Taylor, 1986: 44)

Paul Taylor is arguing, as we saw in an earlier section, for an 'ultimate moral attitude' to nature, based on the interdependency of all parts within the whole (including human life) which cause us to talk in terms of a "whole earth community". So the integrity of the biological system has an element of intrinsic goodness. This goodness is, as Hursthouse points out, based on an Aristotelean idea "any living thing has a **TELOS** - a good of its own - as such, any living thing can be benefited or harmed" (2006:163).

Hursthouse takes up this point about the link between virtue and the place of the earth community to argue for two new virtues: respect for nature and a "sense of wonder". Taylor, interestingly, draws his inspiration from Kant who sees respect for persons as persons as the foundation for his second formulation of the **CATEGORICAL IMPERATIVE**, "do not treat people simply as a means to an end but always also as an end in themselves". Can this not be extended to a more universal, less anthropocentric (human-centred) formula (which of course, is exactly what Kant fails to do), to respect nature as nature? That is certainly one argument for establishing an environmental ethic.

Hursthouse argues, however, that only virtue ethics can identify and inculcate these right attitudes to nature. Only virtue ethics can supply the motivation to be moral that Kantian ethics lacks. This is because a virtue is set within the whole of life and is a lifetime quest of creating good habits. The habits are linked to the richer goal or telos of a thriving, flourishing planet. In this way virtues motivate us and guide our conduct towards the environment. But this involves a revolution in our naturally anthropocentric (human-centred) values.

> *Coming to see oneself as sharing a 'common bond' with all living things would involve a radical change in our perceptions and emotions, of one's reasons for action and one's action. (2006:163)*

In other words, Hursthouse argues that virtue ethics can supply the motivation that Kantian ethics or utilitarianism lack. For virtue ethics goes one stage back, as it were, in arguing for virtues inculcated from childhood in the training and development of character. She argues that this can be done if we reorientate eduction around some core skills which help children identify what actions 'harm' or 'kill' or 'cause pain' or 'feed' as linked to the proper purpose of the living thing in question and identification of certain **NATURALISTIC** features of our behaviour

A practical example might help to ground this idea. Suppose I see a child pulling a cat's tail. The first step is to establish that this causes pain (a naturalistic feature of the action of tail pulling). The next step is to link the action to the vice of cruelty. So we might argue "don't pull Tabby's tail, it's cruel!'. We have given a reason to justify a rule which would be followed by the virtuous person: "don't pull tails".

How could this be applied as an idea to the larger issues of climate change and pollution? Many people assent to the idea that "pollution is wrong". But does this guide actions in a practical way? Take for example, the Glastonbury festival (my example, not her's), brimming with environmental idealists. How many tons of litter are picked up at the end of the festival? How many caravans, tents, bicycles are simply abandoned and therefore wasted? This would seem to give force to Hursthouse's argument that we need to teach new virtues and vices in such a way that they become second nature (not to waste, not to pollute with litter).

A second virtue alongside the respect for nature, she argues, would be a sense of wonder. This is linked to a proper appreciation of beauty within the environment. My respect for a tree stems from an appreciation not just of the place of the tree in the ecosystem (see above) but the inherent goodness of a tree's beauty. This beauty is not just to do with appearance, though it includes that, but in the beauty of its function - it's ability to recycle carbon dioxide as the earth's lungs, and to generate oxygen which sustains all life. Such reverence for nature, an ability to feel awe, could again be inculcated by education at an early age - if only we could move education away from its instrumental, means to an end obsession with attaining some target of exam success.

In other words, if all of us meditated hard on our contribution to educating and practising the virtue of wonder, we could develop the practical wisdom to "feel wonder in the right way, towards the right objects, for the right reasons, to the right degree, and to act accordingly" (2006:161). And would we thereby change our practices? Would such character formation change behaviour at pop festivals or in the way we choose a new car or way we drive it? Of course the answer is "yes", for that is the strength of the idea of virtue - it gives reasons and it forms motives which help alter character and guide practical action.

Two interpretations of Virtue Ethics

As in previous sections I offer two possible interpretations of Virtue Ethics and its approach to the environment. Remember it depends partly on which version of virtue ethics one considers. Aristote orientates his theory of the virtues around habits that build a flourishing life by the exercise of right judgment. That right judgment or **PHRONESIS** judges the golden mean which lies between two vices, that of excess and that of deficiency.

MacIntyre in contrast argues that virtues inhabit certain forms of life. So the virtues are relative to practices, what he calls 'goods internal to practices'. Family practices produce one set of virtues, such as patience and compassion, and business practices another, such as responsibility, honesty and fidelity. Each practice will have relative to it a different set of practices. MacIntyre rejects Arsitotle's view that everything has a proper cause or telos and the ultimate cause of human beings is to reason well. In Aristotle's metaphysical system, the soul has two parts, the rational and the non-rational. The role of the virtues is to bring the non-rational part under the control of reason. How do the two contrary interpretations work?

▶ Interpretation 1 - virtue ethics is not useful in coming to decisions about the environment

Taking Alasdair MacIntyre's account of the virtues in After Virtue it could be argued that virtue ethics is a form of moral relativism as it ties habits of character to **FORMS OF LIFE**. These moral goods are 'internal to practices' MacIntyre argues. So family life has its own set of moral values, as does business ethics. The value only makes sense within the practice, much as the rules of cricket only make sense within the game of cricket.

The difficulty here lies in constructing an environmental ethic. Which form of life are we talking about? In the form of life of business there would appear to be a pragmatism because if a business fails to make profit, it ceases to exist. Moreover, managers fear most of all two things: failing to satisfy shareholders who may call for their dismissal, or being taken over by another company as the share price drops, which almost always ensures a new management team is put in. Competition inevitably forces business to seek lower and lower costs - itself an incentive to exploit third world labour forces.

So depending on the virtues we select as appropriate to our form of life, we may find different views of the environment emerging. The virtue of conservation, in addition, can conflict with the virtue of loyalty and compassion for my family. The extinction of species such as the northern white rhino in Africa is driven by the economic need for poaching among very poor people, and the demand in Asian countries for white rhino horn which is believed to have medicinal properties.

Such beliefs which drive markets are themselves culturally relative and show how the virtues may struggle to establish a strong ethic of responsibility or respect for nature.

▶ **Interpretation 2 - virtue ethics is the most useful method of coming to a decision about issues surrounding the environment.**

In a brilliant TED lecture professor Barry Schwartz explains how it is only through developing the skill of right judgement (**PHRONESIS**) that human beings can show the kind of flexibility of thinking to make wise judgements in a complex world. Tracing this skill to Aristotle he argues that Virtue Ethics teaches us how to combine moral will and moral skill. The virtues of courage and tenacity help us practise the skill, and the virtues of compassion, sympathy and honesty give us the will.

The virtues are character traits we develop through emulation (copying good heroes), education (seeking to understand the virtues) and experience, where the mistakes and triumphs we experience are reflected upon and used to sharpen our wisdom. The end result is what Aristotle calls **EUDAIMONIA**, a state of being where we are fulfilled and our characters blossom into excellence.

How can this process help us exercise right judgement over the environment? As Rosalind Hursthouse explains, we discover the importance of new virtues which are adaptable to the conditions and circumstances of the age we live in. The supreme goal of personal and social flourishing remains fixed, but the means to achieve this goal may vary. These key virtues themselves are not fixed: to Aquinas they are the virtues of faith, hope and love, and to the Greeks, the four virtues of justice, temperance, courage and wisdom (the practical wisdom mentioned above).

Neither Aquinas nor Aristotle, living in an age of a stabler climate with less potential to pollute and degrade the environment, and without the pressing problems of a world population estimated to peak at 11 billion in 2100, could foresee the need for virtues which reverenced the natural world. Hence Hursthouse suggests the virtues of wonder and respect for nature be developed in us so as to appreciate more fully the interdependence of all life on the planet, and cause us to take a less instrumental view of how to use the earth's resources.

By avoiding hard and fast rules (the problem of Kant's categoricals) and also bypassing the short-termism of utilitarian ethics, virtue ethics may provide a way of agreeing on social norms and conventions which will help to establish the reverence for our world, its beauty and wonder, and our proper place within it.

CHRISTIAN ETHICS

Humans have been actively shaping the land for millennia: changing agricultural production, clearing forests and breeding new genetic strains of species of animal for food production. Our actions have had long term unintended effects on the biosphere. However, following the industrial revolution, use of technology has meant that our power over nature has intensified and now includes the power to change the chemical composition of the earth by use of fertilisers and pesticides.

Lynn White, in an article in 1974, accuses Christianity of being the most anthropocentric religion the world has ever seen, and of bequeathing values which work against the environment.

> *Man named all the animals, thus establishing his dominance over them. God planned all of this explicitly for man's benefit and rule: no item in the physical creation had any purpose save to serve man's purposes. (White, 1974)*

We have seen that one source of a Christian environmental ethic is Natural Law which stresses human reason and the proper function and purpose of human beings. But this second strain of Christian ethics is drawn from the Bible and is closer to Protestantism. In the Bible, the source of a view of dominion lies in Genesis, with the word 'kabash' meaning to tread down.

> *Be fruitful and multiply and fill the earth and subdue [kabash] it and have dominion over the fish of the sea and over the birds of the heavens and over every living thing that moves on the earth. (Genesis 1:22, 28)*

White points out the elevated status of human beings: 'although man's body is made of clay, he is not simply part of nature: he is made in God's image'. Humankind is created at the pinnacle of creation, just a little lower than angels. The created world is a gift of God to human beings and so Christian teaching 'established a dualism of man and nature but also insisted that it is God's will that man exploit nature for his proper ends'. White concludes that 'we are superior to nature, contemptuous of it, willing to use it for our slightest whim'.

Lynn White also concedes that a countermovement developed, led by St Francis who 'tried to depose man from his monarchy over creation and set up a democracy of all God's creatures'. The 'whisper' of some enlightened individuals, who treated all nature equally worthy of God's faith, hope and love, was suppressed by church leaders who thought it smacked on animism and paganism.

> *The greatest spiritual revolutionary in western history, St Francis, proposed what he thought was an alternative Christian view of nature and man's relation to it; he tried to substitute the idea of the equality of all creatures, including man, for the ideas of man's limitless rule of creation. He failed. (White, 1974)*

In recent years the concept of **STEWARDSHIP** has been revived with its implication that we nurture creation held in trust as stewards of what is beautiful and good. As the Oxford Bible commentary puts it: "It does not mean exploitation; for food or any other purpose; rather it is a consequence of the gift to mankind of the image of God. Mankind is, as it were, a manager or supervisor of the world of living creatures." (2001)

So God is the owner and true ruler of the earth (Ex. 9:29, 19:9; Is. 45:12). Yet, alongside this thought, as Psalm 115:16 states, "God has given the earth to man." Because God has given humans nature and the earth as gifts, they should honour God with their use of it. Humankind has two complementary roles: to subdue and till the earth, but also to care for it. This is part of our true worship.

Humankind also has a **RESTORATIVE** role. Nature has been cursed by the Fall of Man; weeds grow, and it is our role to bring restoration of the earth through our management: Jesus Christ is redeemer (restorer) of both the physical and spiritual aspects of God's creation. According to Paul, we await this great restoration at the end of time:

> *The creation waits in eager expectation for the sons of God to be revealed. For the creation was subjected to frustration, not by its own choice, but by the will of the one who subjected it, in hope that the creation itself will be liberated from its bondage to decay and brought into the glorious freedom of the children of God. (Rom. 8:19-21).*

In recent years an environmental theology has developed in which theologians such as Francis Schaeffer stress that "the Christian who believes the Bible should be the man who - with God's help and in the power of the Holy Spirit - is treating nature now in the direction of the way nature will be when Christ returns." (1970:45). This environmental theology, supported by other writers such as Norman Geisler, argues forcibly for the stewardship principles of using and caring, both of which are derived from God's commands and the idea of creation as "good".

Christians are called by God both to work (till the land) and care (it is very good) and a proper view of environmental stewardship arguably requires an emphasis on both, based in God's creation ethic. However Lynn White may be right that in society and some parts of the Christian community, environmental views still predominate that set humankind above nature. These distortions include materialism and a dualistic

Christianity that sets mankind against nature. His critique is compelling, especially when viewed against the slow response to western nations to the evidence of climate change.

> *No new set of basic values has been accepted in our society to displace those of Christianity. Hence we shall continue to have a worsening ecologic crisis until we reject the Christian axiom that nature has no reason for existence save to serve man. (White, 1974)*

Lynn White calls on Christianity to find a new idea of humanity and its relation to the created world.

Business Ethics

The words 'business' and 'ethics' are sometimes considered to be mutually contradictory. Business, it might be argued, is about profit and maximising value for the owners of the business (the **SHAREHOLDERS**) whereas ethics is about right living and right values - values such as justice, fairness and equality. The very conjunction of the two words also begs some questions: is Business Ethics a separate branch of ethics? Or is it about applying the ethical theories we have learnt to how businessmen and women behave?

In the following chapters I give my own answers to these questions and adopt an approach which links the key theories on our syllabus to the issues surrounding business ethics. I adopt a case study approach, linking Kant to a case study on Enron, Utilitarianism to a case study on the Ford Pinto, Natural Law to Erin Brokovitch and Virtue Ethics to Trafigura.

Of course, you can take additional examples such as the Banking crisis of 2007, the Bhopal disaster in India in 1986 or the relation of suppliers of cheap goods (such as Primark) and the place of low-paid workers in third world countries. I will mention these briefly - a more in-depth analysis can be found in the resources section of the website.

THE ISSUES IN BUSINESS ETHICS

There are a number of issues raised by our study of business ethics, and we will address each of these six issues in turn in subsequent sections of the book. My own view, which I will develop here, is that business ethics needs to be considered as a separate branch of ethics because companies have a unique status in law: they are fictitious entities which function in law as if they were persons. In other words. companies have an interest quite separate from the people who work in them. This makes sense, as company staff come and go, but it comes as quite a shock to us to find the strength of this concept in company law.

There is a second reason that we should treat business ethics as separate subject. Companies claim to have an **ETHOS** or character. I say claim, because the ethos presented in various mission statements and value statements of a company don't always reflect the values which the company actually practices. Your school is a company of sorts - think of its mission statement and its core values. Are these embodied by those who work in the school? Or is it another kind of fiction, a moral fiction, a smokescreen to try and convince everyone that it is a moral entity?

Additional material and new cases will be added to the accompanying website in order to keep the ideas fresh and relevant. I will also try and make sure that any developments in my own thinking is reflected in additional material which will be made available. But for the moment, what are these issues we need to address?

1. How do we define business ethics?

2. How does business ethics relate to issues surrounding **GLOBALISATION**, the interconnected global market and the free movement of capital and labour?

3. How does business ethics relate to the **PROFIT MOTIVE** and a model of economics first developed by Adam Smith (called the neoclassical model and further developed by Milton Friedman)?

4. What is meant by '**STAKEHOLDER THEORY**' and 'corporate social responsibility' (developed by writers such as Edward Freeman) and how does this concept of moral responsibility relate to business practice?

5. How does business ethics relate to the five models of ethics usually considered by students - the Utilitarian model, the Kantian model, the Natural Law model, the Virtue Ethical model and the Christian ethical model?

6. Finally, how does business ethics handle issues surrounding the environment raised by our previous chapters?

DEFINING BUSINESS ETHICS

In 1968 Albert Carr wrote an article 'Is Business Bluffing Ethical?" arguing that business is not subject to the same ethical standards as the rest of us, but operates by rules equivalent to a game of poker, where bluffing and lying were perfectly permissible. He argues:

> *Poker's own brand of ethics is different from the ethical ideals of civilised human relationships. The game calls for distrust of the other fellow. It ignores the claim of friendship. Cunning deception and concealment of one's strength and intentions, not kindness and openheartedness, are vital in poker. No one thinks any the worse of poker on that account. And no one should think any the worse of the game of business because its standards of right and wrong differ from the prevailing traditions of morality in our society. (Albert Z. Carr, "Is Business Bluffing Ethical?" Harvard Business Review, January/February 1968).*

Carr sees business in other words as a kind of game where you play by shifting rules - a relativistic world where absolute moral standards cannot apply. Yet in recent years new models of business behaviour have emerged and new ethical ideas. These as we shall see appeal to moral theories and elevate the idea of business duty above business self-interest. One such theory Is the stakeholder theory of Edward Freeman, considered in detail below.

But as Crane and Matten observe 'even what we might think of as bad ethics is ethics of a sort' (Crane and Matten, Business Ethics, OUP page 4). As business relationships are in the end human relationships, it must mean that if trust, fairness and honesty never existed then business relationships would be impossible. Perhaps there is a set of absolutes which must logically exist for a business to flourish and thrive. If so the debate needs to begin: what are these absolute moral standards? Can corrupt businesses ever truly flourish?

Crane and Matten go on to offer us this fairly straightforward definition:

> *Business ethics is the study of business situations, activities and decisions where issues of right and wrong are addressed.*

Indeed the ethical foundation of business is reflected in the UK Companies Act 2006. Here the company is described as being like a person - to be cared for in the best interest of that person. So directors have what are called **FIDUCIARY DUTIES** in law - these are duties held on trust - duties towards each other as well as the company itself. They even have duties towards their creditors.

> *A director of a company must act in the way he considers, in good faith, would be most likely to promote the success of the company for the benefit of its members as a whole, and in doing so have regard (amongst other matters) to -*
>
> *(a) the likely consequences of any decision in the long term,*
>
> *(b) the interests of the company's employees,*
>
> *(c) the need to foster the company's business relationships with suppliers, customers and others,*
>
> *(d) the impact of the company's operations on the community and the environment,*

(e) the desirability of the company maintaining a reputation for high standards of business conduct, and

(f) the need to act fairly as between members of the company.

A director of a company must exercise reasonable care, skill and diligence. (2006: sections 172-4)

So on this particular point I disagree fundamentally with Crane and Matten when they imply that ethics begins where the law ends. As a point of fact, UK company law is based on common law principles of honesty, fairness and compassion for the other person. UK law appears to take a Kantian view of ethics - that we should treat the other person as if we were that person ourselves, that we should 'have regard to the other person's interests'. This may be somewhat surprising, and indeed, it makes the development of business case law difficult because no two situations are alike, but it does indicate that as far as UK business law is concerned, the law clearly relates moral principles and hence expects all business personnel to uphold the highest standards of rightness.

Yet on another point I agree with Crane and Matten. Business ethics does inhabit a grey area where we need to decide where two moral principles conflict, what we are to do, or where we are asked to do something, such as provide a bribe to secure a contract overseas, which we might find morally dubious and illegal if such a situation occurred in the UK, how we are to think. These conflicts are the everyday stuff of businessmen inhabiting a world of corrupt regimes, dictatorships, and governments which fail to provide a basic structure of the rule of law. Should companies exit such markets or try to navigate their way through an ethically murky world? If they exit such markets, can they really be said to be putting the interests of their shareholders and employees first?

GLOBALISATION

Businesses exist in global markets where information exchange and commercial transactions occur at the touch of a computer keyboard. The nature of this global market place was revealed in dramatic fashion in the global financial crisis of 2007-9. In his autobiography, Alister Darling reveals how the Royal Bank of Scotland was within six hours of folding, and how he flew back from a meeting in Portugal formulating a bailout policy from the air. The reason for this is simple: risks have increased with the speed of market movements and uncertainty spreads quicker and more widely than ever before.

Globalisation also implies a global market in labour. Firms pursuing low-cost solutions to drive profits upwards may locate in areas of the world where wages are low, safety standards poor and hours long. The human cost of this was brought home to us in 2013 when a factory, the Rana Plaza, manufacturing cheap clothing for UK consumers, collapsed in Savar, Bangladesh, killing 1,219 people and injuring 2,515. Their customers included Walmart, Primark, Bennetton and Mango - some of the best known brand names on UK high streets. Cracks had appeared in the building the day before and workers were told to go back to work or face the losing of a month's pay. Many paid for this obedience to an unjust command with heir lives.

Pope Francis commented a few weeks later:

> A headline that really struck me on the day of the tragedy in Bangladesh was 'Living on 38 euros a month'. That is what the people who died were being paid. This is called slave labour. Today in the world this slavery is being committed against something beautiful that God has given us – the capacity to

create, to work, to have dignity. How many brothers and sisters find themselves in this situation! Not paying fairly, not giving a job because you are only looking at balance sheets, only looking at how to make a profit. That goes against God!

Furthermore, globalisation implies that countries have organised into transnational blocks. The EU, for example, was founded in 1957 and now comprises 28 countries, with new members (such as Turkey, Montenegro and Serbia) queuing to join. In 1993 the Single Market was established with 'four freedoms' at its heart: freedom of movement of goods, services, people and money. Two treaties, the 'Maastricht' Treaty on European Union in 1993 and the Treaty of Amsterdam in 1999 underpinned a move towards closer co-operation on the environment and defence. The Schengen agreements are gradually allowing people to travel without having their passports checked at the borders. Michael Scholte has described this process by the ugly word 'deterritorialisation' which implies that national borders have less and less significance.

To this definition of globalisation as deterritorialisation Indah Wahyuni (2005) adds another four:

1. **INTERNATIONALISATION** - an intensification of cross-border interactions and interdependence between countries.

2. **LIBERALISATION** - a process of removing government-imposed restrictions on movements between countries in order to create an 'open', 'integrated' world economy.

3. **UNIVERSALISATION** - the spread of various objects and experiences to people at all corners of the earth.

4. **WESTERNISATION** - the dominance of one culture, and one language, especially in an Americanised form.

BUSINESS ETHICS - TAMING THE PROFIT MOTIVE

Adam Smith is described as the father of Economics, writing the first Economics textbook in 1776, The Wealth of Nations. In truth he is the father of a certain view of the world of commerce, one that elevates the market and the market mechanism as the best way to arrange commercial transactions. Smith argued for what he calls a 'natural system of liberty' where

> *Every man, as long as he does not violate the laws of justice, is left perfectly free to pursue his own interest his own way, and to bring both his industry and capital into competition with those of any other man, or order of men. (WN IV.ix.51).*

Adam Smith coined the phrase **THE INVISIBLE HAND** for a way of looking at this commercial world where free producers exchange goods and services with free consumers. The invisible hand is a mechanism whereby prices rise and fall according to demand and supply. Put simply, if there are more people wanting to buy something than sell that thing, then prices will rise. As prices rise, more sellers are attracted into the market until at some point buyers and sellers equal each other. In this idealised theory it is the consumer who decides, by allocating his other income votes, which goods and services are produced and hence how resources are allocated. Market economics calls this **CONSUMER SOVEREIGNTY**.

Clearly there is some validity in this view of the world, particularly the world that Adam Smith inhabited. However, there are also a number for problems with it for the world of twenty-first century commerce.

First of all, our economic activity is dominated by large corporations which cross national boundaries - **MULTINATIONAL**

CORPORATIONS. Companies like Google, McDonalds, Nike, Coca-Cola are household names and they operate in nearly every country in the world. Moreover, it could be argued that there are networks of power whereby just a few very large banks, for example, control the activities of the entire world banking system.

In 2011 a team at at the Swiss Federal Institute of Technology in Zurich identified a core of 1318 international banking companies that had direct ties of co-ownership with on average 20 other companies. They estimated that these companies earned 60% of global corporate revenue. Pursuing a deeper analysis, they discovered just 147 super-companies which were especially dominant. James Gattfielder concluded that 'in effect 1% of companies were able to control 40% of the entire network" (New Scientist, October 2011).

This interconnectedness can have moral implications. If large corporations collude together on prices, or use their multinational status to avoid tax, then it has implications for all of us. Starbucks coffee chain was one of many companies accused of doing just that. To a globalisation protester, this interconnectedness may be evidence of a conspiracy by the rich against the poor, but for the rest of us the implications may be economic. When one bank collapses, the others can follow like a pack of cards - and that might have been the terrible outcome of that day in 2008 and when Alistair Darliing had just six hours to act to save the Royal Bank of Scotland.

Secondly, large corporations have what we call **MONOPOLY POWER**. They can determine not just the price consumers pay (which can be overinflated for reasons of profit) but also the wages that workers receive. To what extent are large companies like Primark responsible for the low wages and poor conditions of their Bangladeshi suppliers? Do they have a moral responsibility to audit these suppliers and insist on minimum standards? If these minimum standards are applied they will mean higher prices for Primark's customers. Can Primark act alone if other clothing companies don't follow the same ethical practices? These are the kind of complex questions suggested by the interdependent world in which we live.

And thirdly - Adam Smith assumed a world of perfect information where consumers know everything. We might think this world exists today with the rapid dissemination of information over the internet. Yet when we think more deeply the very existence of the internet raises moral questions. People assume fake identities, and advertisers attach brand features to a product which bear little relation to the product itself. We also follow trends often in an unreflective way - we all join Facebook together and then switch to Twitter en masse. In other words, we are much more open to manipulation in this interconnected world than we ever were, and this raises questions itself. With freedom comes responsibility - but just how free are we? To imply as Adam Smith did, that the consumer is somehow sovereign is to take a very optimistic view.

Milton Friedman and the profit motive

A modern advocate of the views of Adam Smith and the benefits of free markets is Milton Friedman, the father of a certain view of free market economics called **MONETARISM**. In his book Capitalism and Freedom, Milton Friedman appears to take an extreme view on the question of corporate responsibility , arguing in effect that businesses have one responsibility which is to make profits.

> *In a free economy there is one and only one social responsibility of business, to use its resources and engage in activities*

designed to increase its profits so long as it stays within the rules of the game, which is to say, engages in free competition and avoids deception and fraud. (1962:133)

Friedman suggests that corporations should therefore specialise in what they are good at - making money - and leave moral rules to Governments. But he doesn't, we might note, exclude all moral rules : those rules required for the proper functioning of markets such as honesty and freedom are elevated above other rules. This freedom includes the freedom to form companies, to trade and to own shares which are seen as extensions of the property rights of a free society.

In this concern for certain moral principles which strengthen market systems and which are also generated by market systems (such as freedom) Friedman follows Adam Smith. But critics of both Smith and Friedman often overstate their case. Adam Smith advocated principles of justice and fairness as well as espousing the free actions of the market:

No society can surely be flourishing and happy, of which the far greater part of the members are poor and miserable. It is but equity, besides, that they who feed, clothe and lodge the whole body of the people, should have such a share of the produce of their own labour as to be themselves tolerably well fed, clothed and lodged. (WN I.viii.36)

And Milton Friedman argues strongly that certain moral principles, such as honesty, legal enforcement fair contracts and property rights, underpin the market system. Without these elements of morality there can be no fair market.

We can conclude, therefore, that there is a place for ethics even in the more extreme versions of free market economics.

STAKEHOLDER THEORY

A stakeholder can be defined as anyone who has a stake in the success or failure of a company. There can be a narrow or a wide definition of stakeholders. Milton Friedman, for example, the father of Monetarism, would make the frame of reference narrow, including just four groups: suppliers, employees, shareholders and customers. A wider definition, the network view would embrace Local Government, the local community, and even competitors. It is interesting that the UK Companies Act includes fiduciary duties even to creditors, which may be the bank that has lent you money. The Act therefore seems to cast the net of stakeholders fairly widely, and to insist on standards of firmness, care and consideration which on first reading seem surprising to us.

So supporting Freeman's view, we can see that UK legislation confirms that companies have duties to a wide selection of people, and are required in law to consider their interests. It is simply not true to imply, as Milton Friedman does, that companies need only have ethical concern for relatively few people, nor is it true to say that the ethics of companies purely relate to the functioning of markets. So where Friedman implies that deception is wrong because it upsets the smooth transmission of information necessary for markets to function (such as clear contracts at clearly stated prices), UK law suggest that a much wider range of stakeholders must not be deceived. As mentioned above, we cannot, for example, deceive someone who has lent us money into thinking that we cannot pay them back when in fact we can.

However, a word of caution here. The experience of the financial crisis of 2007-9 demonstrates how easily the banking system evaded legal requirements to be prudent over their lending, and developed complex financial instruments to spread risk around the global network. The new financial regulator, The Financial Services Authority, created in 2001, was clearly not up to the challenge of understanding the very complex relationships it was empowered to regulate. Northern Rock (the first bank in the UK to fail in 2007) had, in a drive to be top mortgage lender, produced mortgage loans which were 110% of the property value. In other words, if we were buying a house for £100,000, Northern Rock was willing to lend us £110,000.

This is fine if we assume house prices will continue to rise, but should they be stagnant or fall then the Bank is left with a liability it cannot afford and the rational thing for the borrower to do is to post the keys through the letterbox and pass the liability back to the bank. In a nutshell, that is why banks began in 2007 began to fail.

Stakeholder theory may make not just moral sense but commercial sense. It may be a rational strategy in a market of environmentally savvy consumers to advertise the extent of a company's ethical concern. A company which takes its environmental ethic seriously is more likely to thrive because consumers want companies that have green credentials and a company that treats its employees with dignity and respect is more likely to gain loyalty and hard work in return.

So Edward Freeman (1984) crisply defines his stakeholder argument thus:

> My thesis is that I can revitalise the concept of managerial capitalism by replacing the notion that managers have a fiduciary duty to shareholders with the view that mangers have a fiduciary duty to stakeholders.(1984:39)

Invoking a Kantian concept of treating people not just as means, but as ends, he continues:

Each of these stakeholder groups has a right to be treated not just as a means to an end and therefore must participate in the future direction of the firm in which they have a stake.

There is evidence, I argue here, that UK company law supports this hard view of corporate obligation, but that the law does nonetheless, as the banking crisis proves, not always prove able to protect us.

Corporate Social Responsibility

This idea, derived from stakeholder theory, implies that corporations have responsibility not just to their owners (shareholders) but to wider society. But this begs the question; why do they have this obligation, and where does it come from?

1. **PRAGMATISM** - Companies may see it as good public relations to have an ethical perspective - and consumers may be increasingly demanding it.

2. **RECRUITMENT** - Companies with clear guidelines and practices of social responsibility are more likely to treat their employees fairly and consider their interests. This becomes an attractive feature when recruiting new workers.

3. **LEGISLATION** - Companies which behave better avoid having new regulations imposed on them. For example, the newspapers involved in the phone hacking scandals of recent years signed up to a voluntary code of practice in order to avoid Government legislation.

4. **IDEALISM** - Anita Roddick, founder of Body Shop, pledged from the very beginning to source products free from animal testing. She also pledged to give a proportion of profits away every year to support an Amazonian tribe, the Kayapo indians, whose nut oil is used in its rainforest hair conditioner. Such idealism does exist in corporate behaviour: it stems from idealism because the brand benefit comes later.

It may be possible, in addition, to measure corporate social responsibility in terms of policies, outcomes and stated values. New 'ethical company' indexes are gradually emerging. For example, in the UK there exists the FTSE4good index. This assesses company performance against a number of criteria, including employment policy, environmental impacts and anti-corruption measures. A fuller list of criteria can be found by consulting the ethical corporation criteria in the Business Ethics section of the website.

Four Ethical Models of Business Behaviour

The study of ethics usually begins by examining four ethical models: Utilitarianism, Kantian ethics, Natural Law, and Virtue ethics. In this section we will examine each model and apply it to a specific case study to try to answer the question: how do different theories address issues of moral responsibility, and moral conflict which we normally explain with the phrase 'moral dilemmas'?

FORD PINTO - UTILITARIANS ETHICS AND COST-BENEFIT ANALYSIS

Some managers (for example in the Enron case discussed below) are knowingly crooks. But others it would seem slip into behaviour which looks very suspect when viewed from the standpoint of history. They may, or may not, be good people themselves, but the climate of corporate decision-making and the framework of law itself can encourage such behaviour. One such case is Ford Pinto.

In 1968 Ford Motor Company, led by Vice-President Lee Iacocca, designed a new small family saloon called the Ford Pinto. They rushed it into production because of fears that competitors were about to do the same, as the normal time taken to produce a new model is about 43 months and the Pinto took just 25. Unfortunately it also had a fairly serious design fault: when shunted up the back, the fuel tank exploded into flame and risked serious injury or even death to the occupants. The design fault was known to Ford, but only revealed to the buying public in 1977.

Now one way of assessing news of such a fault is to apply cost-benefit analysis. With **COST-BENEFIT ANALYSIS** you take the cost of a recall and set it against the likely benefits in lives saved. To do this, you need a calculation of what a human life is worth and a statistical view of how many deaths and injuries are likely to occur. Ford estimated 180 deaths, 180 serious injuries and around 2,000 burnt out cars, at a cost to the company of around £49m and set this against the estimated cost of a recall of £137 m. The net benefit to the company of doing nothing came to £137m - £49m = £88m. So the decision was to do nothing.

Notice this is a variation of Benthamite utilitarian calculation. You take the pleasure and then deduct the pain from your own perspective, assess the likely consequences, and decide to do the pleasure maximising thing by a **HEDONIC CALCULUS**. When pleasure is translated into dollars, you have the kind of thinking the Ford management came up with. What's wrong with this approach to business ethics?

1. It takes a god-like view of consequences. What actually happened was that Ford was sued in the US courts and in one case alone in California, $128m of damages was awarded (that's almost three times the total cost of damages that Ford was estimating). Ford also faced a corporate manslaughter charge which did terrible things to its reputation. As in utilitarian ethics, we cannot truly determine the final costs (the consequences) with any accuracy.

2. It takes a human life and puts a monetary value on it. But it seems unethical to us to turn a tragic death into a monetary figure. What is the cost of a human life?

3. The amount of human suffering involved in such deaths and injuries is probably incalculable as it includes not just the victim,

but also friends, relatives, dependents. What view a judge and jury take of damages is notoriously difficult to prejudge as it depends so much on the individual case.

Ford had an interesting defence which has generated further case law in the US, and many changes to American corporate behaviour. They argued in court that US law encouraged such a cost-benefit approach, as the National Highway Safety Administration had issued guidelines on product recalls which appeared to state that a company is excused from making a recall if the monetary costs of making a production change were greater than the "social benefit" of that change. So the very principles of US law seemed to encourage the sort of unethical behaviour we see in the Pinto case. The Courts, however, took a different view.

ENRON - KANTIAN ETHICS AND THE IDEA OF DUTY

We have seen that the UK Companies Act of 2006 places 'fiduciary duties' at the heart of Company Law. These are duties owed to all stakeholders to behave honestly, fairly and as far as possible considering the interests of all parties. A core duty (which even free market advocates like Milton Friedman accept) is not to deceive or deliberately lie. In the complex fraud that became known as the Enron Scandal of 2002, deception came to light on a grand scale which destroyed not just Enron itself, but the leading accountancy firm Arthur Andersen.

Enron was founded in 1985 and grew rapidly, winning awards as a leading innovator. Its core business was energy supply, but it expanded into a number of other areas, such as insurance and video streaming. At the same time, it had a reputation for sacking 20% of its workforce every year - placing a burden on employees to engage in sometimes dubious practices in the energy market.

The energy malpractice came to a head in California. It emerged that from 2000 to 2001 Enron traders created artificial shortages of electricity which led to power cuts across California. Enron employees arranged deliberate power plant shutdowns 'for maintenance'. As prices rose due to the shortage of power, traders sold energy at inflated prices and boosted profits. There appeared to be a callous disregard of the effects of power cuts on public welfare.

The financial fraud was complex. It included new accounting procedures that allowed Enron to record paper profits, that is, profits that didn't yet exist. Current income became mixed up with projected income which wouldn't be realised for a number of years.

In addition, Enron created shadow companies known as Raptors. This enabled them to shift money around and take debts off the main company's balance sheet. In other words, the level of debt was itself disguised. The share price of the parent company (higher than it would otherwise have been) was then used as security for the debt of the smaller companies, so that as long as Enron share price rose, everything was fine. But if the share price fell below some point, then Enron could collapse like a pack of shady cards.

When the company Managing Director, Jeff Skilling resigned in August 2001 it gave the opportunity for a whistleblower, a Vice president Sherron Watkins, to report on what seemed to be complex web of fraud. As the declared losses began to mount up, Enron filed for bankruptcy in December 2001. By 2006, Skilling was serving a 25 year jail sentence for corporate fraud and Arthur Andersen, Enron's accountancy firm, had ceased to exist.

One of the central principles of Kantian ethics is the idea of the 'good will'. This means that every action is ruled by a good motive - a specific type of intention. The key to this good motive is universalising your behaviour so that you place yourself in the other person's shoes. If it doesn't feel good to be in the shoes of a Californian citizen in the middle of a blackout, then don't do the action because it cannot be 'willed as a universal law' - you wouldn't want to be that person yourself.

In addition, Kant argued forcefully by the **FORMULA OF HUMANITY** that 'we should treat people not just as a means to an end, but as end in themselves'. No Enron employee should ever treat any person, such as a consumer of electricity merely as an end to greater profits. Kant argued for a categorical duty to follow the moral law. No matter how much pressure an employer places you under, the imperative is to stick to the moral law because this is the only way the greatest good is served. If more Enron employees had the moral courage to act out of the good will according to Kantian maxims, it is unlikely that the many people who suffered under the malpractices of 2000 to 2001 would have experienced the blackouts, loss of pension fund money and unemployment .

Who knows, but if more employees had had the courage of the whistleblower Sherron Watkins perhaps Jeff Skilling would have changed his mind and now be enjoying the fruits of his honest labour somewhere on a Caribbean beach.

ERIN BROKOVITCH - PACIFIC ENERGY AND NATURAL LAW ETHICS

While a single mother of three working as a legal assistant, Erin Brokovitch (wonderfully portrayed by Julia Roberts in a film of the same name) was working as a researcher at a small town law firm in Hinckley, California. She noticed something odd about the activities of the energy giant Pacific Gas - they were trying to buy up houses in an area where they'd laid a gas pipeline and built storage tanks. Moreover, the health of the residents seemed to feature as part of the negotiation of sale.

The result was a class action - a form of collective lawsuit - against Pacific Gas and Energy citing serious health problems (cancer among them) in residents affected by the toxic chemical chromium 6. Cooling water from a gas compression plant had been dumped in a pool and seeped into the water supply. Hinckley residents, it seems, had been drinking poison for years.

The company settled in 1996 for $333m, the largest ever collective lawsuit. Even in 2013 chromium 6 was appearing again in the water supply of victims of the 1996 seepage - the town of Hinckley was dying itself as residents, losing confidence, sold up and left. Roberta Walker, the main inspiration for the film, was asked in 2013 what she thought of the film:

> Oh, it was a piece of crap. The only true thing about the movie is that Pacific Gas and Electric poisoned us. We didn't bring a giant to their knees, obviously; we just woke them up -- woke up the dragon," (Interview with Miles O'Brien, March 14th, 2013).

There are many such cases of large corporations behaving irresponsibly in the face of health concerns of workers, residents or consumers.

Fearing the consequences of a revelation on their balance sheets, companies are tempted to engage in deception and concealment. In the case of Pacific Gas, they wanted to bury the issue under an area of bulldozed housing, and hoped the sick, often with lifetime of health problems, would simply go away.

What does Natural Law ethics say about cases such as this? Natural Law theory, such as that developed by Thomas Aquinas and then adopted as the primary moral philosophy of the Roman Catholic Church, is based on the Greek teleological worldview. This sees the ultimate goal to be a state of personal and social fulfilment, flourishing or welfare called **EUDAIMONIA**. Eudaimonia is sometimes translated as happiness but is better seen as a long-term organic growth into the best state we can achieve, given the natural conditions of our life.

Unlike utilitarian ethics, which at least with Benthamite hedonism seems to collapse into selfish egoism, the goal can never be narrowly conceived because to the Greeks, the personal and social dimensions are interlinked. Aristotle, keen as he was on virtues that built the flourishing life, saw clearly that social virtue was as important as personal virtue. It is as important to pursue justice as it is to develop perseverance in the face of difficulty. And Virtue Ethics and Natural Law share this common goal or ultimate telos of eudaimonia.

According to Aquinas, natural law is the human expression of the eternal law of God that is woven into the very fabric of the Universe. God is a God of loving purposes and we can see this as we observe the Universe. When it comes to humans the thing that sets us apart is our rationality - human beings have the ability to reason well and to share in the mind of God, to think God's thoughts with him - and so the natural law is the sharing by intelligent creatures in the eternal law of God.

Human beings are born with an innate, designed-in sense of right and wrong, argues Aquinas. He calls this **SYNDERESIS**. This is the natural tendency we have to pursue good rational ends. Of course we could deliberately choose something else, but we always, so Aquinas thought, at least believe we are doing good by our rational choice. Aquinas would have to be charitable to Pacific Gas and argue that even they believed that by buying the houses they were maximising the welfare of the community - tarmacing over the problem and persuading them to move away. And when the community includes the workers and the shareholders, as stakeholder theory, you can see how they might rationalising their behaviour as 'maximising welfare for all stakeholders'.

From this starting point of an inbuilt desire to reason towards good ends, Aquinas argues that we reasonably pursue five primary goods, or precepts: we seek to preserve life, to reproduce, to educate ourselves, to worship God and to live in society. This latter precept explains again the social dimension of Greek ethics where the good of the individual is inextricably linked to the good of the community where we live.

The problem with Natural Law theory, however, is that where the primary precepts are supposed to be absolute, unchanging, universal expressions of our rational natures, **SECONDARY PRECEPTS** are merely human interpretations of these general precepts, or as Aquinas puts it, 'proximate conclusions'. This is both a strength and a weakness. It means Natural Law theory can adapt readily to insights from modern science, insights of biology or of psychology for example. But it also means it is open to debate whether any particular action is a valid or invalid application of a primary precept. For example, it is quite possible for me to disagree with the Roman Catholic interpretation of contraception because I argue that preservation of life In Africa through the use of condoms outweighs the mandate to reproduce, which is hampered by the use of condoms.

Might Paciifc Gas have wriggled out of an ethical debate using a particular interpretation or secondary principle derived from the primary goods of Natural Law? Could they have argued they were putting 'living in society' above 'preservation of life' for example? I don't think so. My own belief is that Natural Law possess within it a hierarchy of value so that preservation of life trumps other precepts. In other words, if any precept comes into conflict with the precept to preserve life, it is the other precept (as I would argue happens with contraception) which has to give way. We cannot just live with a clash of two goods without resolving the clash in favour of one or the other. To do otherwise is to duck out of true moral debate.

So Pacific Gas was acting wrongly according to Natural Law, for at least three reasons.

- Firstly, it did not connect community eudaimonia, community welfare, to its own actions in the way that Natural Law insists we should.

- Secondly, it clearly broke the moral obligation to preserve human life and protect from harm.

- Thirdly, it practised deception in way that violated the key principles of living in society - the need to be honest, to build trust with each other and to consider the interest of others alongside and even above our own. Moreover, they sought to escape justice even when the leak was discovered, by offering a payout of $40m to settle out of court.

- Pacific Gas and Energy are condemned therefore in the moral court for actions that broke the Natural Moral Law in a number of places (which after all is something which is at the heart of the US Constitution which states   'these rights to be inalienable").

TRAFIGURA AND VIRTUE ETHICS

Trafigura is a large multinational company that trades in oil, based in Holland. In 2006 a ship, the Probo Koala, chartered by Trafigura, docked in Amsterdam, requiring its tanks to be cleaned out and the toxic waste disposed of. Those tasked with cleaning the hold had filled the tanks with caustic soda which they tried to pass off as 'harmless slops'. They then decided that the cost of cleaning the toxic cargo in Amsterdam was too high, and so arranged for the waste to be removed to the Ivory Coast - at a much cheaper price but arguably with the risk that the waste, in a country of less rigorous cpntrols, would be illegally dumped. That's exactly what happened, and allegedly the toxic gas hydrogen sulphide was released into the environment of Abidjan.

Villagers in the area began to fall ill with respiratory problems, and according to a report commissioned by the firm:

> Among the side effects listed death as well as severe burns to the skin and lungs, vomiting and diarrhoea. (BBC, October 17th, 2009)

It is possible that 17 people died, and around 100,000 people experienced side effects as a result of the illegal dumping. In 2007 1,000 Ivory Coast citizens began a collective action against Trafigura, who eventually agreed to a $160m out of court settlement, without admitting liability. Trafigura also paid $50m (£32m) in an out-of-court settlement to individuals in Ivory Coast who said they had been injured when the waste was spread on dumps around Abidjan. The company claimed that the people who did the dumping, who were not employees of the company, were acting of their own initiative. The individuals eventually received lengthy jail terms.

This case raises interesting moral questions. Can a company be held responsible for an action it didn't directly authorise? Does a company have a responsibility for its own toxic waste beyond the confines of its own ships, or its own jurisdiction? Are you guilty if some consequence might have been foreseen by a reasonable person, taking everything into account? And who pays the external cost of pollution and of illness resulting from commercial activity which occurred many miles away?

Virtue Ethics argues that it is character that it is the source of moral actions, and therefore that ethics is by its very nature agent-centred. It is the agent's character, including motives, emotions, beliefs and values which determines the decision taken. It is a holistic theory which places integrity as the supreme value - a wholeness and integration of character towards the goal or telos of eudaimonia, the flourishing life.

As with Natural Law theory, the idea of virtue emerges in Greek ethics in the fourth century BC. Aristotle, for example argued that "The happy life is thought to be one of excellence (Greek **ARETE** or virtue); now an excellent life requires exertion, and does not consist in amusement. If Eudaimonia, or happiness, is activity in accordance with excellence, it is reasonable that it should be in accordance with the highest excellence (virtue)". Virtues are organic - they are grown by activities within a person as result of three influences. We emulate (copy) the characteristics of our heroes, we experience good and bad choices and reflect upon them, and we are educated by parents, schools and our peer group into a 'good life'.

Virtues therefore can be seen as skills for life. The word arete in Greek means both skill and virtue. So Wayne Rooney can be seen as a virtuous (skilled) footballer because he has perfected the art of curling a free kick. Nelson Mandela can be seen as a virtuous person because he exhibits certain character traits - honesty, perseverance, courage, reliability, compassion and graciousness, for example.

Aristotle argued that these character traits require one supreme intellectual virtue - **PHRONESIS** or practical wisdom. To Aristotle phronesis means right judgement, which is an 'activity of the soul in accordance with virtue'. This virtue of phronesis means we reflect on things, events, consequences, effects on other people and we modify our behaviour according to those values (virtues) which we honestly think will build a flourishing life and a flourishing community. In employing this idea of right judgement Aristotle argued we choose a golden mean between two vices - the vice of deficiency and of excess.

Take courage for example. Courage lies somewhere between the deficiency of courage, which we call cowardice, and the excess of courage, which we call recklessness. This mean point should not be thought of as a point of moderation but as a point of right judgement. For example, courage implies acting with the right amount of courage in the right situation in the right sort of way. Sometimes it may involve doing something very risky and at other times, courage demands that we hold back. It just depends on the circumstances how courage translates into action.

Virtue ethics has much to teach those involved in business. Companies operate as fictitious persons, as we have seen, a concept enshrined in UK law. Companies present an 'ethics' (Greek for character) in their mission statements and statements of values. Trafigura, for example, has strong values as the company clearly declares:

> We apply skill, market intelligence and worldwide resources to add value for our customers and stakeholders and optimise the value chain. We act responsibly in all our markets. Our focus is

on long-term investments and lasting relationships. (Trafigura website)

Because companies are large and complex organisations, it isn't quite possible that employees believe and act according to these values, but that one rogue employee can bring the whole corporate ethos into disrepute. It is also quite conceivable that Trafigura knew nothing about the toxic gases released by a subcontractor disposing of the waste in a way they saw fit in the Ivory Coast.

Virtue Ethics however demands we put integrity first. That means we do not lie, deceive, conceal or pretend things are not the case when they are. These vales cannot build a flourishing market system, as the market economist Milton Friedman makes clear, let alone a flourishing life. Did Trafigura attempt to conceal the truth? I leave you to investigate this for yourself, but it is clear that Panorama, the Guardian newspaper and the MP who raised this issue in the House of Commons, and who were threatened with legal action for defamation, would have a view on this and they themselves required moral courage to continue the investigation.

Indeed, the Guardian looked back in pride at their own investigation in an article in 2010.

> *If Guardian News & Media were to highlight one investigation over the past year that would sum up our core values of "honesty, integrity, courage, fairness, and a sense of duty to the reader and the community", it would have to be our exposure of Trafigura.*

> *The Guardian gained international recognition for its part in bringing to light the behaviour of the firm of offshore oil traders*

whose cheaply-dumped toxic waste poisoned thousands of Africans. The Guardian saw its initial legal battle to publish escalate into a full-scale constitutional crisis, because the wealthy corporation's lawyers tried to stop the paper reporting proceedings in the British parliament.

Trafigura obtained a superinjunction, banning the Guardian not only from revealing the contents of a leaked scientific report, but also even from disclosing that the company had gone to court to get such an injunction. The Guardian, and ultimately, many politicians and members of the public, saw this as a Kafkaesque assault on free speech, which had to be defeated, (Guardian, July 6th 2010).

In this way the ethos of a company can indeed reflect the ethos of all of us.

Conclusions

The argument here has been twofold. In the case of environmental ethics, we need either to find a source of intrinsic goodness, or to rehabilitate traditional theories to accommodate environmental concerns. Sources of intrinsic goodness include respect for nature, placing value on diversity, and redefining humanity as part of an interdependent system rather than an overlord of a pyramid of value. We need to examine the arguments for intrinsic goodness and ask whether they are compelling,

In the case of business ethics, I have argued that it is legitimate to see business ethics as a separate discipline for two reasons. Firstly, UK company law treats the business itself as an entity with interests that must be protected by the fiduciary duties of directors. These are duties held on trust to operate in the best interests of the business itself and all **STAKEHOLDERS** - a Kantian idea that those stakeholders should be treated as ends in themselves.

Secondly, businesses profess to have an ethos, a set of characteristics expressed in its mission statements and statements of value. Of course, as we found with the Trafigura case study, what employees and contractors end up doing and negotiating on behalf of the business may not correspond to these values, and the question then arises: should the business originating (in this case) the pollutant be held responsible?

In this final chapter I revisit the four questions which lie at the heart of every attempt to understand and evaluate moral theories. They spell the acronym **DARM**.

DERIVATION - HOW IS GOODNESS DERIVED (OR DETERMINED)?

In traditional theories of ethics goodness is derived by a process of human reason, using the human perspective as primary. Thus Kantian ethics adopts a process of **A PRIORI** reason, standing back from the situation and universalising by an act of imagination to create categoricals, universal laws which create duties for all mankind. Modern Kantians stress that Kantian ethics can be adapted to generate **INDIRECT DUTIES** to the environment, whereby the duty exists to care for the environment because of what value that gives indirectly to the idea of human good.

Utilitarian ethics stresses the desirability of pleasure and the undesirability of pain. Hence **SENTIENCE** - the ability to feel - is the key moral criterion of value. Pleasure is good, pain is bad. We have seen how Peter Singer takes this idea and applies it to animals. Following Bentham he argues that it is wrong to allow animal suffering. But although the environment can be included more generally in our moral calculation, it is included only instrumentally insofar as it adds to (through its beauty) or detracts (through climate change) from human happiness generally.

Natural Law ethics also begins with an innate ability to reason well, known as **SYNDERESIS**. Rational beings by nature desire to do good and avoid evil, and humans possess an intuitive grasp of primary precepts. These are good things that yield a life of **EUDAIMONIA** - of fulfilment and positive welfare. Preservation of Life has always been top of this list. But it is also true that animals have generally been seen, as in Aquinas' writing, as a means to an end, the end of food. However, I have argued that Natural Law theory could take another approach: by invoking the idea of the Eternal Law (which could be linked by a nonbeliever to some idea of Platonic perfection) Natural Law theorists could create a stronger set of environmental laws and duties.

But what of intrinsic goodness? The search for a source of intrinsic goodness comes up against two problems. One is that the ascribing of value is itself a human process. If we say **RESPECT FOR NATURE** is intrinsically good, this implies that there is something in nature itself worthy of our respect that we can point to and which can be agreed upon. What is that thing?

One value might be beauty. But then not all nature is beautiful and beauty is a somewhat relative idea. Mountains used to be seen as sinister and forbidding before the romantic revival, led by William Wordsworth, changed our perception. And again, some natural processes are evil in their effects: volcanoes, tsunamis and hurricanes for example.

So the second problem is this: the natural world is only partially good, when we link the word 'good' to some common feature such as 'life-enhancing'. Viruses, some bacteria, and even the activities of some animals can be seen as requiring regulation to bring their destructive effects under control. To talk then of 'intrinsic goodness' isn't as simple as we might think - witness the furore over the badger culls in Somerset, where people are disagreeing about whose suffering (the cows', the farmers', the badgers') matters most.

APPLICATION - HOW DO WE APPLY THE IDEA OF 'GOODNESS'?

Having decided what the quality is that has goodness, we then have to apply it to human behaviour and pass laws about it. Let's suppose we can agree that **BIODIVERSITY** is intrinsically a good thing, and a loss of diversity a bad thing.

As often happens in ethics, this appears to be straightforward until we try to apply the idea. Within the natural world, numbers of species have fluctuated with natural climate cycles. I say 'natural' because historically huge fluctuations in climate have occurred in periods of warming and cooling. Accepting for a moment the theory of Darwinian natural selection, those species that have adapted have survived and those that have failed to adapt have died. Neanderthal man died out 50,000 years ago (possibly due to a failure to co-operate as well as homo sapiens). Homo sapiens have thrived.

However a basic conflict of interest exists today between homo sapiens and the natural world. As the populate increases, more resources will be employed simply to feed the growing populations. Stocks of fish will be depleted, animals hunted to extinction and forests cut down. To appeal to some idea of intrinsic goodness is irrelevant when your own life is threatened. Human beings will always tend to choose life, human life over animal and plant life, should it be a matter of life and death.

Faced with such pressure it's hard to see where an appeal to the 'beauty, integrity and diversity' of the biosphere, or a 'respect for nature' takes us. Such a value of goodness may be difficult or impossible to apply.

REALISM - IS THE VALUE TRUE TO OUR SHARED NATURES?

Because of these twin problems, the problem of finding a compelling idea of intrinsic goodness and the problem of applying any such value, philosophers such as John Passmore have argued that we need to adapt anthropocentric theories to produce an idea of **ENLIGHTENED ANTHROPOCENTRISM**.

Take, for example, utilitarian ethics. This can be adapted to include the environment because environmental degradation is clearly in nobody's best interest. The problem is, however, that egoistic forms of utilitarian ethics that simply add up every individual's perception of their own happiness, fail to address what Garrett Hardin calls the tragedy of the commons. This, roughly speaking, means that if everyone grazes common land based on their own individual utility, the land generally gets grazed to extinction. The tragedy of the commons is that no-one perceives the overall effect of dropping one crisp packet at the Glastonbury festival - that ten tonnes of rubbish accumulate in a way I would never tolerate if it was my own back garden.

Theories of ethics have to be realistic and appeal to human nature. This was Mill's point when he elevated education as the source of moral learning and also stressed **SYMPATHY** as the key virtue that builds the moral life. We care about other humans, about animals, even about the environment because we sympathise with the plight of the dolphin caught in a fisherman's net, the white rhino killed for its horn, even the rainforest with its beauty destroyed by deforestation.

It may be that in a version of Mill's so-called weak **RULE UTILITARIANISM** we can generate long term duties set by our own collective wisdom alongside short-term calculations of what compromises are needed to save human life.

MOTIVATION - WHY SHOULD I BE MORAL?

Finally, we come to a most pressing problem: how do we convince human beings to follow a moral norm we have carefully established as benefiting some idea of the common good?

Consider business ethics. In 2009 the Banking system came very close to collapse as Northern Rock and Royal Bank of Scotland could not meet their obligations and pay their bad debts. Bankers were accused of greed, taking huge bonuses and then extraordinarily big risks with savers' money. They were accused of acting in the knowledge that no Government would allow the bank to go bankrupt, and they themselves, the directors, would escape liability. This proved to be correct. No director has been jailed for their recklessness.

But why should a director of a bank pursue a wiser, more moral path today? One argument might be that they do it for prudential reasons. Customers demand higher ethical standards, and Governments might pass legislation to make directors more liable for their recklessness. This, of course, is another version of utilitarian **CONSEQUENTIALISM**. We make the consequences so painful that behaviour gets re-adjusted.

Interestingly, not all banks follow the same commercial logic. Banks in the Netherlands, such as **FORTIS** bank, have traditionally followed a much more ethical stance. This may be because the recognise that duties articulated and then fulfilled to their customers and the wider community has commercial logic.

But it may also be because they have thought long and hard about ethics. Because, at the base position of all ethical theories is the view that if we all follow the moral path, everyone wins. Human life, biotic life, the environment can at least in theory grow and benefit together as each protects the interest of the other, and those parts of the interdependent system which cannot think and reason are nonetheless given value - whether it is **INSTRUMENTAL** value or **INTRINSIC** value, the effect will arguably be the same.

Suggested Reading

- **ATTFIELD, R**. (2014) Environmental Ethics: An Overview for the Twenty-First Century (Polity)

- **CALLICOTT, JOHN BAIRD**, in Jamieson ed., (2003) A Companion to Environmental Philosophy (Blackwell)

- **CRANE, A. AND MATTEN, D.** (2006) Business Ethics: Managing Corporate Citizenship and Sustainability in the Age of Globalization (OUP)

- **DES JARDINS, JOSEPH, R.** (2000) Environmental Ethics: An Introduction to Environmental Philosophy (Wadsworth)

- **GREY, W.** "Anthropocentrism and Deep Ecology", Australasian Journal of Philosophy 71: no 4, December 1993.

- **HARDIN, G.** (1968) The Tragedy of the Commons (Science, 13, vol 162)

- **HARGROVE, E.C.** The Animal Rights Debate: the Environmental Perspective

- **JONES, C. PARKER, M. TEN BOS, R.** (2007) For Business Ethics (Routledge)

- **KORSGAARD, C.** (1996) Creating the Kingdom of Ends (CUP)

- **LEOPOLD, A.** (1968) A Land County Almanac and Sketches Here and There (OUP)

- **LOVELOCK, J.** (2000) Gaia: A New Look at Life on Earth (Oxford)

- **LOVELOCK, J.** (2007) The Revenge of Gaia (Penguin)

- **LOVELOCK, J.** (2010) The Vanishing Face of Gaia (Penguin)

- **PASSMORE, J.** (1974) Man's Responsibility for Nature (Duckworth)

- **PYRA, L.** The Anthropocentric Ethics of John Passmore versus the Biocentric Ethics of Paul Taylor

- **REGAN, T.** (2004) The Case for Animal Rights (University of California Press)

- **SCHAEFFER, F.** (1970) Pollution and the Death of Man. (Hodder & Stoughton)

- **SHIRK, E.** (1998) New Dimensions in Ethics: Ethics and the Environment

- **SINGER, P.** (1995) Animal Liberation (Pimlico)

- **SINGER, P.** (2011) Practical Ethics (CUP)

- **TAYLOR, PAUL W.** (1986) Respect for Nature (Princeton)

- **TYRRELL, T.** (2013) On Gaia: A Critical Investigation of the Relationship between Life and Earth (Princeton U.P.)

- **WAHYUNI, I.F.** (2005) The Challenge for Translators in Globalization. International Conference on Translation. (Sebelas Maret University Press)

- **WHITE, MAR D** (2011) Kantian Ethics and Economics (Stanford)

- **WHITE, LYNN.** (1974) The Historical Roots of our Ecological Crisis (New York :Harper and Row).

- **WOOD, ALLEN** (2007) Kantian Ethics (CUP)

Lightning Source UK Ltd.
Milton Keynes UK
UKOW07f2123031214

242607UK00001B/1/P

9 781909 618268